I0830664

THE
BREAKING
OF A
NEW DAWN
An Anthology of Prophetic Words
Concerning Nigeria
JOSEPH OLA

From

· ·

To

· ·

Date

· ·

THE
BREAKING
OF A
NEW DAWN

*An Anthology of Prophetic Words
Concerning Nigeria*

JOSEPH OLA

THE BREAKING OF A NEW DAWN

AN ANTHOLOGY OF PROPHETIC WORDS
CONCERNING NIGERIA

JOSEPH OLA

Word Alive

CONTENTS

1. *Young and Found: A 40-Day Devotional for Young Adults and Teens*
2. *Pandemic Joy: Making Sense of Life's Uncertainties*
3. *Marriage in View*
4. *Is This Opportunity From God?: 7 Checkpoints for Discerning Divine Opportunities*
5. *#Unaddicted: Finding Freedom from Sex-related Addictions*
6. *Bumpy But Sweet (A Love Story)*
7. *Waiting Compass: Finding God when He seems to delay*
8. *Alive: Living in the Power of Grace and Truth*
9. *The Salvation Journey*

*Details about these titles are available on the last few pages of this book

Dedication

*To the memory of two generals with a keen sense of Nigeria's prophetic destiny: **Pastor Sydney G. Elton** and **Pastor Emmanuel Olatoye.***

Pa S.G. Elton (as he was fondly called) was a missionary to Nigeria sent by The Apostolic Church of Great Britain in 1937. He was the first Area Superintendent of The Apostolic Church Nigeria in Ilesa (1937-1954) after which, as a freelance pentecostal minister, devoted himself to identifying, raising and mentoring indigenous pentecostal and charismatic ministers until his death in 1987.

Pastor Emmanuel Olatoye lived his latter years in the UK with an unrelenting passion to birth a new Nigeria through prayers. We never met physically but he reached out to me in 2018 after reading my compilation of prophecies about Nigeria posted on Facebook in 2010. I had since been on his mailing list for his 'Pray for Nigeria' activities. He passed away in September 2020 right in the middle of leading a 40-day prayer for Nigeria. May His soul rest in peace.

ACKNOWLEDGMENTS

The anthological nature of this work necessitates that I rely on the voices, words and works of many channels through whom God has been communicating about His Mission — *missio Dei* — on earth. It is befitting that I celebrate them.

Massive thanks to: Ayodeji Abodunde for his brilliant biography of Pa S.G. Elton; Dr Tony Rapu for his still-relevant 2002 article titled "A Call to Order"; Pastor Olubi Johnson for his insightful location of Nigeria in the scriptures and his beautiful book *I am Black but Comely*; Dr Ruth Marshall for her comprehensive book on Nigerian Pentecostalism; 'Intercessors for Nigeria' for archiving God's prophetic words for Nigeria over the years; Pastor Debo Adesina for always sharing prophecies for Nigeria curated from different sources; Gbenga Richmond for his book,

Grineria; Dr Harvey Kwiyani for telling us about the 'Blessed Reflex' in his books — *Sent Forth* and *Multi-cultural Kingdom*; Dr Richard Burgess for researching into the missional agenda of Nigerian pastors in the UK, Dr Joseph Olowe for his revelatory book on Nigeria and many other sources that had been cited in this anthology.

I will also like to thank Pastor Olaoluwa Okunnuwa for editing this piece and Emmanuel Olude for volunteering to design the cover — and delivering with excellence! May your labour of love never go unrewarded.

To my lovely wife, Eleos, and our boys, Joshua OdodoOluwa and Samuel OkikiOluwa, thanks for always allowing me to sneak out of the room in the middle of the night to do things like this.

And to You, O Lord, be all the praise for we are persuaded that You watch over Your Word concerning Nigeria to bring it to pass.

PREFACE

Ọjọ́ kì í pẹ́ tÍtÍ kó má pèé; ọjọ́ kì í jìnnà jìnnà kó má kò.
The future is never so distant that it does not arrive.
— a Yorùbá Proverb

This book was put together in light of the October 2020 protests in Nigeria and is intended to be a prayer guide for the well-meaning Nigerian and anyone interested in the prophetic destiny of the country. To borrow the words of the writer of the epistle to the Hebrews,

"Throughout our history God has spoken to our ancestors by his prophets in many different ways..."

— (HEBREWS 1:1 TPT)

My sensitivity to God's prophetic agenda for Nigeria came about in 2009. I was writing an article intended to be published on Nigeria's 49th Independence Anniversary when I stumbled on an article about the Nigerian flag which made me really curious. An excerpt from the article—written by Whitney Smith —is as follows:

> Work toward independence led to the establishment of a national planning committee, which in 1958 called for a competition to select a national flag. Almost 3,000 designs were submitted, many of great complexity. The winning design was by **Michael Taiwo Akinkumi**, a Nigerian student in London. In his flag of equal green-white-green vertical stripes, **green stood for Agriculture and white for Unity and Peace**. The original design also included **a red quarter sun on the white stripe as a symbol of Divine Protection and Guidance, but this was omitted by the committee**. ...It is typical that Nigeria, like many other culturally diverse countries, chose a simple flag design.[1]

I couldn't resist reading a spiritual meaning to that discovery. Why would anyone choose to delete the symbol of divine protection and guidance from a national flag? Where is the Sun now? (Or better asked, "Where is the Son?") Would an additional piece of significant symbol make a flag complex? (Has anyone seen the flag of Turkmenistan?)

Ever since this discovery, I have become more intentional with praying for the nation and more aware of God's prophetic word concerning the nation.

In 2010, I compiled some prophecies concerning the nation most of which were sourced from the then website of *Intercessors for Nigeria.* I continued to pray with those words. In 2011 when I participated in the National Youth Service Corps (NYSC) in Gombe State, Northern Nigeria, I felt very much like a part of a fulfillment of prophecy. The NYSC, by the way, is indeed a fulfilment of prophecy spoken by Pa S.G. Elton who came to Nigeria in the early 1930's as a British missionary. He was moved by the Spirit of God to prophesy that

> a time will come when the Nigerian Government would be paying her Youth to preach the Gospel in all nooks and crannies of the country.[2]

This prophecy tarried for some time and looked like it will not come to pass. However, the Biafra War of 1967 to 1970 set the pace for the fulfillment. In the year 1973, during the regime of General Yakubu Gowon, in a bid to build one united Nigeria, he established the scheme that is now known as **NATIONAL YOUTH SERVICE CORPS (NYSC).** This scheme demands that young Nigerian graduates be posted to states other than their state of origin to serve their nation in order to foster unity. 10 years into the scheme (in 1983), the **NIGERIA CHRISTIAN CORPERS' FELLOWSHIP (NCCF)** came into existence. This fellowship became a missionary arm of the NYSC in a sense. Young Christians serving the nation in every state around the country will make intentional efforts to reach the unreached in their respective states. They engage in what is called *rural rugged evangelism* among other initiatives. In my time at Gombe state, we went on missionary journeys into Y'Deba, Kaltungo, Dukku and many other interior villages in the North-East of Nigeria. It was a memorable experience walking in prophecy fulfilment and being involved in God's end-time agenda.

In 2012, on completion of my NYSC year, I sensed a persuasion to embrace a lifetime call into pastoral ministry. My ministerial journey commenced in the same denomination[3] in which my parents raised me — The Apostolic Church Nigeria. It was a journey into an unknown future. One of the peculiar assignments of TACN, it turned out, was a prophetic responsibility to continue to pray for Nigeria. No Sunday service ended without this assignment being carried out. As such, I stayed in touch with my sensitivity of a prophetic destiny for Nigeria. I followed every major election since then quite keenly.

In 2015, Providence brought me to the UK to study in a Bible and Leadership College in Bradford (Life Church College). My programme at Bradford opened up the opportunity to pursue a Masters Degree in Biblical and Pastoral Theology at Liverpool Hope University. In the course of my dissertation in which I researched the limitations facing African-Pioneered Churches in the UK, I found out that I was in the midst of yet another dimension of prophecy fulfilment. These were prophecies that had been given about Africa (and Nigeria being central to the continental vision) long before the amalgamation of the protectorates that will become known as Nigeria in 1914. (I say more about these prophecies in Chapter 1).

I retrace this journey about my sensitivity to God's prophetic agenda concerning Nigeria to make a point. The God that fulfilled the prophecy that Pa Elton gave about Nigerian youths and the prophecies birthed by the ministry of William Carey and Edward

Blyden (shared in Chapter 1) is still in the business of fulfilling His counsel in our days. That God has continued to speak persistently concerning our Nigeria is an indication of His undying love for this nation as well as His immutable counsel to use this nation for His glory. A little wonder therefore that the hordes of hell have continued to launch the fiercest assaults available in the domain of darkness at this nation so richly blessed and endowed by God. All of satan's orchestrations against the nation in the past 60 years have been his frantic efforts to hinder the fulfilment of God's prophetic mandate over her. Our responsibility as members of the Body of Christ is to position ourselves strategically for the fulfil-ment by waging a good warfare in the spirit and taking practical actions that will take us further into the realisations of these time-tested prophetic words.

I have shared the prophecies, largely, *as is*. I cited my sources as much as possible. I refused to comment on the prophecies and trust that the Holy Spirit will minister to us about them; helping us judge them aright and pray with them as we should. I included 4 articles in the epilogue. The first was a befitting tribute to Pa S.G. Elton excerpted from his biography —a brilliant work by Ayodeji Abodunde. The second was written by Dr Tony Rapu (pastor of *This Present*

House) and featured in a book about Nigerian Pentecostalism. I think it is instructive for the nation, still. The third was a sermon by Pastor Olubi Johnson (pastor of *Scripture Pasture Christian Centre*) who had repeatedly located Nigeria in the scriptures and preached God's counsel about the nation. He published a book earlier this year which is a recommended read. It's titled **I am Black but Comely (From Beyond the Rivers of Ethiopia)**. The last is an article I wrote reflecting on the ongoing protests in Nigeria at the time of publishing this book—protests in which many young people have (dare I say, *unnecessarily*) lost their lives. In the article, I share 4 practical principles every Nigerian youth can start applying now to see the birth of a New Nigeria. I hope Nigeria Christian youths find it instructive.

Feel free to share this compilation with your friends and everyone you feel will find it helpful.

One last thing: a request. I intend to continue to update and grow this collection. If you come across any other trustworthy prophecy about Nigeria, feel free to send them my way. My email address is hello@josephkolawole.org. I will be happy to hear from you.

"Nigeria shall rise again", says the Lord. Amen.

1

1792-1888

I thought to begin this collection of prophecies by reiterating one particular prophecy that was made concerning the continent of Africa as a whole regarding her place in destiny to bring revival to the lands and nations that evangelised and brought civilisation to her lands — and God has used Nigeria, especially and significantly, to fulfil this prophecy in striking measures.

THE PROPHETIC SEED PLANTED IN 1792

It began with the work of William Carey in the years leading up to 1800. Specifically in 1792, he published an essay entitled *An Enquiry into the Obligations of Christians to Use Means for the Conversion of the Heathens in which the Religious State of the Different*

Nations of the World, the Success of Former Undertakings, and the Practicability of Further Undertakings are considered.[1] Based on his data collection about the religious state of different nations, he argued that the world out there needed to hear the gospel, and that the English (or European) Christians had to take the gospel to them.

He suggested that a few Christians could easily form an association that could then send and support missionaries to the unevangelized world. And indeed, he convinced his audience that everybody, especially lay members of the Church, should get involved in mission.

He did not only talk, he acted. He formed the Baptist Missionary Society as a model for what he was suggesting. Then in 1793, he left England to become a missionary in India, where he served until his death in 1834. He never returned to England. Then, as Kwiyani articulates it,

In the decades following 1792, the Protestant missionary movement gained great momentum. William Carey's work had opened the way. At the time, less than 10 per cent of world Christians lived outside the West. Yet, as Western missionaries went to evangelize the world (long before the colonial project), even then some spoke hopefully of the day when Christians from those unevangelized lands would come to help invigorate Western Christianity. They hoped for a day in the future when Christianity would grow so strong in Africa and Asia that African and Asian Christians would come to the West to strengthen Western Christianity. They called this phenomenon the 'blessed reflex'.[2]

To understand how illogical it was to think like that at the time, Kwiyani helps us understand the context a bit more:

At that time in the history of Christianity, however, anticipating that some of the people converting to Christianity in Africa or Asia would engage in mission in the very countries that sent them missionaries, even if in theory only, was rather too ambitious. On the one hand, the transatlantic slave trade was yet to be abolished (although this happened in 1806, slave traders still pillaged Africa well into the 1880s and 1890s), so for many Europeans, black and brown peoples of the world were generally yet to be accepted as fully human. On the other, there was no indication that Christianity would thrive in Africa or in Asia. Even a hundred years later, in the early 1900s, there was no guarantee that Christianity would explode around the world as much as it has done. This optimism is hard to justify and, of course, it precedes (and was to be made futile by) much of the colonial expansion of Europe and the dehumanizing of Africans and Asians beyond Western civilization.[3]

THE 1888 PROPHECY FROM EDWARD BLYDEN

Below is an excerpt from my dissertation for my Masters degree in Biblical and Pastoral Theology at Liverpool Hope University in the UK (2017).

African Christianity in Diaspora
(with a focus on Britain)

The idea of Africa playing a central role in World Christianity is not new. In essence, it is a predicted pre-colonisation idea popularised by the likes of **Edward Blyden** in the nineteenth century when he said:

Africa may yet prove to be the spiritual conservatory of the world ...When the civilised nations in consequence of their wonderful material development, shall have had their spiritual perceptions darkened and spiritual susceptibilities blunted through the agency of a captivating and absorbing materialism, it may be that they have to resort to Africa to recover some of the simple elements of faith, for the promise of that land is that she shall stretch forth her hands unto God.[4]

In practice, scattered occurrences of this was ongoing before Blyden's speech. John Jea, an African Preacher was said to have had a fruitful itinerant ministry in North America and Europe and might have started a church in his house around 1805-15 when he settled in Portsmouth with his wife.[5] In the same century, some black ministers were leading white congregations at various moments.[6]

In the UK, in 1906, a Ghanaian businessman and school master, Rev. Thomas Kwame Brem-Wilson founded Sumner Road Chapel in Peckham. This is arguably the first black Pentecostal church in Britain and still exists till date.[7]

In 1930, a notable forerunner of **Nigerian missions in Britain** came on the scene. According to Marika Sherwood,[8] **Daniels Ekarte** (1890s-1964) founded and led *African Church Mission*[9] in 1931.[10] Ekarte was born into the twins-killing town of Calabar, Nigeria where he had been influenced by Arthur Wilkie and Mary Slessor (1848-1915), the Scottish missionary. He arrived in Britain in the year that Mary Slessor died in search of a fresh beginning in his spiritual journey—a journey he reckoned as a pilgrimage only to be welcomed with racial prejudice. Higgins noted that he became so disillusioned that he renounced his faith briefly and was determined to return to Nigeria and denounce the missionaries. His faith was rekindled however, and he went on to take up the challenge of evangelising the land and confronting racism paralleling Mary Slessor's vexation against the killing of twins in Calabar and her initiative in acting against it. In a feedback letter to Arthur Wilkie, his brother who had visited ACM wrote concerning Ekarte's mission work, 'the teaching has performed a whole circle – from Britain to Africa and from Africa back to Britain. It is one of the most striking incidents I have ever heard of in the sowing of the Word.'[11] In this regard, Ekarte arguably qualifies as the first African 'reverse missionary' in Britain. ACM grew rapidly with over 500 people 'registered' in the Mission located in Toxteth[12] within the first three years[13] as the mission met the social and spiritual needs of both Africans and other ethnic minority Liverpool residents in the racially tense atmosphere of Ekarte's day. The mission, however, was cut short due to an unrelenting institutional racism and lack of funds. The mission agency was forcefully shut down by the local authorities in 1964, and shortly after in the same year, Ekarte also died.

In the 1960s shortly after the Windrush generation (1940s-1950s) and about the same time when many African countries gained independence, the 'great European migration'[14] went into reverse as African diplomats, tourists and students migrated to Britain[15] bringing their religion with them.[16] In no time, and consequent to not feeling welcome in the mainline indigenous churches, the proliferation of African Initiated[17] Churches in Britain began.[18] The first of such churches to be planted was the Church of the Lord Aladura (Aladura) founded in 1964 by late Primate Adeleke Adejobi and assisted by Rev. Father Olu Abiola in South London.[19]

The most recent influx of African Christianity into Britain is via the African New Pentecostal Churches (ANPCs) which came on the scene since the 1980s...

Over the years, many of these ANPCs have emerged in Britain and grew at a rate that commanded both scholarly and media attention.

HOW NIGERIA IS FULFILLING THIS PROPHECY — A CASE STUDY OF BRITAIN

Richard Burgess in a journal article titled "Bringing Back the Gospel: Reverse Mission among Nigerian Pentecostals in Britain" reported his research into exactly how Nigerians have been fulfilling this prophecy. This article was published in 2011. We have even more convincing evidence to validate his research ever since. He writes:

If you take a walk down London's Old Kent Road you will encounter what has become a growing phenomenon in Britain, transnational Pentecostal churches from the global South, mainly planted and populated by Africans. Bearing names such as *New Covenant Church, Christ Embassy,* and *Holy Ghost Zone,* they represent an increasingly important addition to the British religious landscape. The 2005 English Church Census showed a steady decline in British church attendance over the previous seven years and the widespread closure of churches from the historic denominations. At the same time over one thousand new churches were opened, a large proportion started by Africans. According to the Directory of Black Majority Churches UK, there are currently 500,000 Black

Christians in Britain and an estimated 4,000 black-majority and black-led churches nationwide. Most are Pentecostal churches and many are founded or led by Nigerians. **Of Britain's ten largest mega-churches, five are led by Nigerians.** (These are Kingsway International Christian Centre, Jesus House, Glory House, Winners Chapel, and New Wine Ministries, all located in London.)[20]

While Britain was the focus of my research at the time, this reality is being observed everywhere in the West today.

We will now turn in subsequent chapters to some specific prophecies about Nigeria.

2

1970-1980

THE "MAP OF AFRICA" VISION BY PA S.G. ELTON

According to the biography of Pa Sydney Elton written by Ayodeji Abodunde, he chronicles a vision which Pa Elton began to share with his listeners in the mid-seventies to the late seventies. He writes,

Elton began to impress upon his hearers the "map of Africa" vision. As far as we know, Elton was the first to give a spiritual connotation to Africa's map, or at the least, he popularized and imprinted its significance in the heart of a generation of Nigerian Christians. **He told them the map of Africa is shaped like a gun and that Nigeria**

was in the position of the trigger. *"There will be trouble in all the strategic points of the gun because the devil will not want God to use Africa as a weapon to shoot into the camp of the enemy. The horn of Africa is the loading point; the devil will trouble this region to prevent the gun from being loaded. The outlet of the bullet—South Africa, is bound by apartheid to prevent the bullet from being discharged, but the outlet will be opened. Nigeria occupies the position of the trigger, and the devil will do all he can [even if the gun is loaded] to stop the trigger from being released."*[1]

3

1983

AT THE NATIONAL PRAYER CONFERENCE OF CHRISTIANS STUDENTS SOCIAL MOVEMENT (CSSM)

This year was the year of the coup that ousted the Shagari Government. The Lord spoke to us as we gathered in prayer in Port Harcourt, not even aware that a coup had taken place.

Son of man say to Nigeria; though you have passed through the valley of the shadow of death, thus saith the Lord, you shall not die but shall live.[1]

AT THE FIRST NATIONAL CONVENTION OF THE FULL GOSPEL BUSINESS MEN'S FELLOWSHIP INTERNATIONAL (FGBMFI) HELD AT HOTEL PRESIDENTIAL IN PORT HARCOURT

A visiting delegate from New Mexico USA spoke about visions of black men that God was giving him while he was in his home country. When he asked about who the black men were, The Lord, he said, explained to him that these black men where Nigerians. He had never visited Nigeria before and the Lord told him he will soon take him there **because the nation Nigeria was a nation he planned to use in revival.** He then spoke on in prophecy:

> Thus saith the Lord: Nigeria and Nigerian Christians will be used by the Lord to preach the gospel in the market places of the World in these last days.[2]

Pastor S. G. Elton spoke prophetically in this meeting concerning two key African nations, saying that

Africa is like a gun pointed down. Its turret and muzzle is South Africa. Its trigger is Nigeria.

He said the days would come when Apartheid (then at its peak in South Africa) will be removed from South Africa. "In those days," he said, "the Gun of Africa would begin to fire for God's purpose."[3]

1984

IBADAN PRAYER CONFERENCE CSSM

As we prayed here at a large gathering of many campuses at the Ibadan Polytechnic, the Lord spoke again during a very deep session of prayers while most of us were on our face on the floor. The Lord spoke in prophecy saying:

My Church in this nation, is My hope for the Continent of Africa.[1]

5

1986

PROPHECY BY LANCE LAMBERT FROM MOUNT CARMEL

This prophecy was given in 1986 in a Prophetic Conference in Jerusalem, Israel. 153 prophets from 30 to 40 nations had gathered to wait upon and to hear from the Lord. The highlights of this prophecy to the entire body of Christ are as follows:

It will not be long before there will come upon the world a time of unparalleled upheaval and turmoil. Do not fear for it is I the Lord who is shaking all things.

I began this shaking with the first world war and I greatly increased it through the second world war. Since 1973 I have given it an even greater impetus.

In the last stage, I plan to complete it with the shaking of the universe itself, with signs in the sun and moon and stars.

But before that point is reached, I will judge the nations and the time is near. It will not only be by war and civil war, by anarchy and terrorism, and by monetary collapses that I will judge the nations, but also by natural disasters: by earthquakes, by shortages and famines and by old and new plague diseases.

I will also judge them by giving them over to their own ways, the lawlessness, to loveless selfishness, to delusion and to believing a lie; to false religion and an apostate church, even to a Christianity without Me. Do not fear when these things begin to happen, for I disclose these things to you before they commence in order that you might be prepared, and that in the day of trouble and of evil you may stand firm and overcome.

For I purpose that you may become the means of encouraging and strengthening many who love Me but who are weak. I desire that through you many may become strong in Me, and that multitudes of others might find My salvation through you.

And hear this! Do not fear the power of the Kremlin, nor the power of the Islamic Revolution, for I plan to break both of them through Israel. I will bring down their pride and their arrogance, and shatter them because they have blasphemed My Name. In that day I will avenge the blood of all the martyrs and of the innocent ones whom they have slaughtered. I will surely do this thing for they have thought that there was no one to judge them. But I have seen their ways and I have heard the cries of the oppressed and of the persecuted and I will break their power and make an end of them.

Be ye therefore prepared for when all this comes to pass, to you will be given the great opportunity to preach the Gospel freely to all nations. In the midst of all the turmoil and shaking, and at the heart of everything, is My Church. In the heavenlies, She is joined to Me in one Spirit and I have destined Her for the throne. You who are My beloved, whom I have redeemed and anointed – you are Mine.

I will equip and empower you and you will rise up and do great things in My Name, even in the midst of darkness and evil. For I will reveal My power, and My grace and glory through you. Do not hold back nor question My ways with you for in all My dealings with you I have always in mind that you should be part of My Bride and reign with Me. Do not forget that this requires discipline and training. So yield to Me that I might do a work in you in the time which is left for I plan even during all this shaking the Bride will make Herself ready.

For in the midst of these judgments multitudes upon multitudes will be saved from the nations. You will hardly know how to bring the harvest in, but my Spirit will equip you for the task.

And to Israel, will I also turn in that day, and I will melt the hardening which has befallen her. I will turn their blindness into clear sight, and tear away the veil on their heart. Then shall they be redeemed with heart bursting joy, and it will become a fountain of new and resurrection life to the whole company of the redeemed.

Do not fear for these days, for I have purposed that you shall stand with Me and serve Me in them. Fear not, for I love you and I will protect you and equip you.

I, the Lord, will anoint you with a new anointing and you will work My works and fulfill My counsel. You shall stand before Me, the Lord of the whole earth and serve Me with understanding and with power and you shall reign with Me during these days. ABOVE ALL, I CALL YOU TO BE INTERCESSORS.

PROPHECY BY PA S.G. ELTON

This prophecy had been shared by many eye-witnesses to it. Some sources put it at 1986 (less than a year before Pa Elton's death), while others simply put it at 'mid-80s'. The following are two versions of the prophecy:

As narrated by Isaac Ezeh

I was in a Christian leadership meeting in the mid 80's where Pa S.G. Elton, a missionary in Nigeria for 50 years, was a guest speaker. Pa Elton was a towering apostolic and prophetic vessel. In that meeting he made this prophetic utterance: *Nigeria and Nigerians will be known all over the world for corruption. Your name — Nigeria will stink for corruption but after a while a new phase will come — a phase of righteousness. People from the nations of the earth will hold to a Nigerian and say, We want to follow you to your nation to go and learn righteousness.*

As narrated by Isaac Ezeh

I was in a Christian leadership meeting in the mid 80's where Pa S.G. Elton, a missionary in Nigeria for 50 years, was a guest speaker. Pa Elton was a towering apostolic and prophetic vessel. In that meeting he made this prophetic utterance: *"Nigeria and Nigerians will be known all over the world for corruption. Your name — Nigeria will stink for corruption but after a while a new phase will come — a phase of righteousness. People from the nations of the earth will hold to a Nigerian and say, We want to follow you to your nation to go and learn righteousness."*[1]

As remembered by Very Rev Dr Deji Okegbile

When 1 was teaching in my beloved home town, Osu, Ilesa (1981-1985), and in my Evangelical Christian Union days in Adeyemi College of Education, Ondo (1986), 1 heard about Pa S. G. Elton who left his native country, England, to come to Nigeria in March 1937 saying *"in the coming revival, Africa is like a hand gun turned downward; Nigeria is the trigger... [and also that] Nigeria/Nigerians will be known for corruption worldwide but the tide will turn and Nigeria will also be known for righteousness worldwide. Many shall take hold of him that is a Nigerian, saying, 'We will go with you, for we have heard that God is with you.'"* [2]

6

1989

EXTRACT, TAPE RECORDED MESSAGE, WEST REGIONAL CONFERENCE, IBADAN (24TH TO 26TH MAY, 2007)

In 1989, on the way to US, I was in Shrewsbury in UK; I met this accountant who had a message given to him in 1983 during the Rivers of Life Conference in East Anglia in UK. The visioner was in a prayer session with his group when God began to show him a vision. God began to show him a vision of countries and lands that was passing through a draught. As he watched God brought him over a parcel of territory that typifies Africa. As he looked on, at a particular portion of that land, that portion was in total darkness, sparks of light was shooting out of that darkness while groaning and cries were coming out of that darkness. As he continues to watch, it appears somebody used a remote control to pause the motion of pictures. At this point he called out to his brethren, he told them that God was showing him something but it seems nothing was moving anymore. His friends told him to keep watching while they pray for him. As soon as they began to pray, it appeared a play button was pressed and the motion came alive again.

Then greater cries were coming out of that land and suddenly there was blinding flash of light that came and swept away that darkness and the whole land birthed with light. God told him that that land he has just seen is called Nigeria. Then they now sat down and began to ask themselves the meaning of this vision. And God told them that **Nigeria is a significant nation in His hands for the establishment of His purposes in the last days, to break the scepter of the religion of sons of the bondwoman, to establish His purposes** and that the principality appointed by Lucifer over Nigeria is in the same category as the principality over Israel and European nations. That is, as tough as it is going to be to fulfill God's purposes. So God told them (this British brethren) to constitute themselves to be interceding for Nigeria. So when he heard from his friends in 1989, that a Nigerian was coming, he came to see me (Steve) and to handover the responsibility. As he finished the message, he said since you are a Nigerian, go home and tell your brethren what God has said. As he finished, he greeted everybody and left.

So it is important to recall what God has said concerning Nigeria. A land covered with darkness in which there were groaning and cries with sparks of lights but needed a great light from heaven to blow away the darkness. It happened suddenly. It will happen suddenly.[1]

— ENGR. STEVE OLUMUYIWA,
NARRATING

7

1990

"CALL TO PRAYER FOR NIGERIA"

In 1990, Pastor Ojewale published a prophetic book about Nigeria titled *Call to Prayer for Nigeria*. In it, Pastor Ojewale claims that the country is on the verge of an unprecedented Christian revival. Indeed, Nigeria has since become the site of Pentecostalism's greatest explosion on the African continent, and the movement's extraordinary growth shows no signs of slowing. Here's an excerpt from the prophetic book:

This is the eve of a national revival. Call it spiritual awakening or revolution if you please. There are few revolutions in history without bloodshed. But there is one revolutionary—the greatest revolutionary of all time—who did not shed another's blood to establish his Kingdom . . . His was a spiritual revolution and it has changed the course of the history of man. . . .

The warfare we are presently engaged in is the battle of translating the victory of Jesus over the devil into the everyday, natural realities of our personal lives and also of our political, religious, economic and social systems. It is a battle of reclamation: to reclaim from the devil what he illegally holds in his control. . . . It is warfare. But we are on the winning side. This is the time to muster the army— the Lord's army. Here is a clarion call to battle. . . .

We are disadvantaged if we lean on carnal weapons. Prayer— militant, strategic and aggressive prayer—must be our weapon of warfare at this time. It is a spiritual warfare and it needs spiritual weapons. This is a call into the ring to wrestle, to sweat it out with an unseen opponent. For we wrestle not against flesh and blood but against spiritual wickedness, against invisible powers in high places (Ephesians 6:12). . . . Nigeria is indeed poised for a revival of an unprecedented dimension. You and I are active participants in what God is about to do. Militant, strategic, unceasing and aggressive prayers will hasten the heavenly visitation. The early showers of revival which many of God's servants have prophesied have begun already. Join the Lord's army to bring about rapid changes that we desperately need in all areas of our national life. We are at the dawn of a new era. I can see it in my spirit. [1]

8

1996

AT IFN, CORE EAST REGIONAL CONFERENCE, ONITSHA

Date: 27th January, 1996

Arise Oh Nigeria! Saith the Lord, Arise from the North, Arise from the South, Arise from the West, Arise from the East. The season of incubation is past. The day to hatch has come and I the Lord bring upon you a visitation, My marked visitation. Even though you have not known Me, yet I have chosen you. In this day I pass through your land in mercy to renew the face of the nations. Even though the nations are despising you, I have desired you as a place for My glory. Therefore, I the

Lord have jealously watched over you to cause My purpose to be done. I have brought you to the valley of decision. There is no time to waste. Arise as a generation for, I have waited for you. I will desire of you genuine dedication. I the Lord will make My demands. But I seek to raise out of you a generation of men who will make My glory known in the ends of the earth. I have purposed it, I will do it. But I ask you to arise. Arise in this day, there is no more time to wait. Arise, Arise, from complacency, Arise from ignorance. Know Me, the God of destiny. Know Me, the God of covenants. For I seek to exhibit you to the world. I have come. This day do I desire a commitment from you. I desire not to wait any longer. My time has come and you shall labour in the nations to bring up children. Therefore, arise into this destiny for the world waits for you, saith the Spirit of the Lord.[1]

AT ARLINGTON VIRGINIA USA ICCC CONFERENCE

At this global Christian convocation of the International Christian Chambers of Commerce (ICCC) held in Arlington VA USA, a white American female delegate called those of us from Nigeria together and intimated us about the word which she said the Lord spoke to correct her view of Nigeria as a nation that was forsaken by the Lord. She said that Lord said He was preparing Nigeria for use in the end time harvest of souls. She said the Lord directed her to go read the entire 36th chapter of the book of Ezekiel. He told her that wherever she saw the name Israel in the chapter, she should put the name Nigeria. The Lord said that way; she will see the full scope of his plan for the nation of Nigeria.

What follows is Ezekiel 36 with 'Israel' replaced with 'Nigeria'

EZEKIEL 36 (VOICE)

36 Eternal One: Son of man, preach to Nigeria's mountains. Tell them to heed the word of the Eternal.

2 Here is what the Eternal Lord has to say:

Eternal One: The enemy rejoiced over you and said, "Finally! The ancient highlands are ours." **3** Because they rejoiced, I, the Eternal Lord, say, "Your enemies crushed you from every side and left you *nothing but* an empty wasteland. They have carried you off *in pieces, divided you up,* and made you a remnant among the nations; and you became the topic of everyone's gossip and malicious attacks."

4 Because of this, you mountains of Nigeria, heed the word of the Eternal Lord. The Eternal Lord says this to the *ancient* mountains and hills, to the riverbeds and valleys, and to the empty wasteland and deserted cities that have been plundered and mocked by every nation around you.

Eternal One: 5 With fiery passion I have spoken against the rest of the nations, *but most especially* to Edom, who with malicious joy took My *precious* land for themselves and divided it up as their spoil. **6** Therefore speak out about the land of Nigeria to the *ancient* mountains and hills and rivers and valleys.

The Eternal Lord gave this message to me.

Eternal One: Look! I have spoken with fiery anger and jealousy because you have been scoffed at by the nations. **7** Therefore, I, the Eternal Lord, lift My hand and swear *to you* that those nations around you *will suffer as you have;* they'll be *mocked and* put to shame.

8 But you, Nigeria's mountains, will shoot forth new branches and bear fruit for My people Nigeria. They will be home soon. **9** I, of course, care about you and will turn My attention on you. Therefore, your soil will be plowed and *your fields* sown. **10** I will increase the population *and replenish* the whole community of Nigeria. I will bring life back into the *desolate* cities, and heaps of rubble will be turned into *grand* structures. **11** I will increase the population of people and animals that live on your slopes once again; they will be more numerous, and you will become more productive than ever before! *After all these things come to pass,* you will know that I am the Eternal. **12** I will settle My people Nigeria on you, and they will possess you, and you will be the land they pass from one generation to the next. You will never again take their children.

13 This is what the Eternal Lord said.

Eternal One: Because some say, "The land of Nigeria is known for devouring its people and depriving them of their children," **14** I declare that you will never devour any of My people again or deprive them of their children. **15** I will see to it that you do not have to listen to the *other* nations scoff at you anymore, and you will no longer suffer humiliation or be the cause of your own nation's faltering.

So said the Eternal.

16 *Again* the word of the Eternal came to me.

Eternal One: 17 Son of man, when Nigeria's people lived in their own land, they desecrated it with their *foul* lifestyles. Their actions were as impure as a woman's menstrual cycle. **18** Because they *infected* the land, pouring out innocent blood and filling *their hearts and* homes with idols, I poured out My wrath upon them. **19** I scattered them among the nations and dispersed them through *many* lands. I judged them based on their lifestyles and actions. **20** Whenever they settled among the nations *of their exile,* they defiled My sacred name. Everywhere they went people were saying, "These are the Eternal's people, yet they have been forced out of His land." **21** I became concerned for My sacred name, for everywhere they went the people of Nigeria were giving Me a bad name.

22 Consequently, tell the people of Nigeria that the Eternal Lord says, "When I act, people of Nigeria, it won't be for your own good, but for the sake of salvaging My own reputation, which you have slandered in front of those outside our covenant.[2] **23** I will restore My great name to its holy state which has been desecrated in every nation by you! *After all these things come to pass and* I reveal My holiness through you right before their eyes, then these nations will know that I am the Eternal. **24** I will take you away from the nations, gather you from all the foreign soils, and bring you back to your own land. **25** I will sprinkle you with clean water, and you will be clean. I will wash away all of your dirtiness, and you will be clean *and pure, free from the taint of* idols. **26** I will plant a new heart and new spirit inside of you. I will take out your *stubborn,* stony heart and give you a *willing, tender* heart of flesh. **27** And I will put My Spirit inside of you and inspire you to live by My statutes and follow My laws. **28** Then you will live in the *same* land I gave your ancestors; you will be My people, and I will be your God. **29-30** I will rescue you from your impurity. I will summon the grain to produce large harvests and never bring a famine upon you *again.* I will increase your harvests of fruit and grain, so that you will never have to face the disgrace of famine again among the nations. **31** Then you will recall your evil ways and wicked deeds. You will recognize how bad they were and hate yourselves for all the shocking and despicable things you did! **32** But I, the Eternal Lord, am not doing this for your own good. You should still feel shame and humiliation for all you've done, people of Nigeria!"

33 This is what the Eternal Lord has to say.

Eternal One: On the day I cleanse you from all your sins, I will bring people back into your *desolate* cities, and heaps of rubble will be turned into *grand* structures. **34** The wasteland will be plowed *and sown*—a vast change from the emptiness those passing by are used to seeing. **35** They will *be amazed,* saying, "This place used to be an empty wasteland. Now it's like the garden of Eden! The cities were *demolished,* lying in ruins and completely abandoned. Now they are *all restored,* strong and full of people!" **36** Then the nations near you will know that I, the Eternal, am the One who rebuilt *and restored* the ruined cities and replanted the empty wilderness. I, the Eternal One, promise to do exactly what I've said.

37 This is what the Eternal Lord has to say.

Eternal One: I will *soothe Nigeria's desire and* do as they have asked Me to do: I will make their population grow like a flock *of sheep.* **38** Just as flocks *of sheep* fill Jerusalem before the sacrifices at the public feasts, the cities filled with rubble will be filled with flocks of people. Then they will know that I am the Eternal One.[3]

— THE VOICE

AT AHOP CONFERENCE, SWAZILAND 1996

Look, you scoffers! Be shocked to death. For in your days I am doing a work, a work you will never believe, even if someone tells you plainly![4]

— ACTS 13:41 (VOICE)

9

―――――――

1998

VISION RECEIVED BY RON SMITH –
PARTICIPATING DELEGATE FROM TEXAS
USA AT ICCC NIGERIA NATIONAL
CONFERENCE HELD AT EXCELLENCE
HOTEL, IKEJA LAGOS ON 12TH
MARCH, 1998

While I was praying at the end of Emeka's message, I saw a vision of a Local Africa Market place. It was looking dirty and filthy. Then the vision changed. I saw the market transformed into a new environment. Gold, diamond and precious stones of various types were stacked neatly and well arranged on a table. I saw an oil font springing up from the table. I also saw in this new market environment, neatly dressed people in three distinct groups: Men, Boys and Babies (little children).

Then I saw trucks full of gold bars moving across the borders of the countries of Africa. I saw a blood stream flowing ahead of the trucks into villages into which the trucks were coming. As the blood stream entered into the villages, it exploded into white light which enveloped the villages. Thus says the Lord,

"There is a wave of prosperity coming from the Lord into Africa. The objective is for the salvation of the peoples of Africa. Idolatry will be overthrown in Africa as part of this move. Beware, however, that you do not replace idolatry with materialism when the release of the wealth comes."

EXCERPTS FROM PROPHECY BY PASTOR
E.A. ADEBOYE AS FEATURED IN J. LEE
GRADY, "NIGERIA'S MIRACLE," COVER
STORY, *CHARISMA*, MAY 2002, PAGE 4

There is no question that the devil was working during the regime of Sani Abacha, the iron-fisted dictator who ruled Nigeria from 1993 until his sudden death in 1998. A Muslim who had aligned himself with military thugs, Islamic radicals and occult sorcerers, Abacha was steering the country toward another war. It is widely known that he asked Islamic clerics to perform occult rituals in the capital to keep him in power. But Christians say God heard the prayers of the church and sent a miracle. It came in the form of Olusegun Obasanjo, a military leader and born-again Christian who had been jailed by Abacha for treason. Like a character from an Old Testament drama, Obasanjo was suddenly plucked from his prison cell and placed in the presidency after a free election in early 1999.[1]

The author of this article credits Pastor Adeboye of the RCCG with having both announced and hastened Abacha's demise.[2]

An invisible spiritual battle raged during Abacha's last days. While he had asked spiritists to bury fetishes, charms and live animals on the property at Aso Rock, Christians were fasting. Meanwhile, **Adeboye, the head of the RCCG, prophesied on June 6, 1998, that God was about to bring a 'new dawn' to Nigeria. Abacha died of a heart attack three days later.**[3]

10

2000

SOUTH AFRICA, APRIL 2000

Yet it is ten years and I would have changed the face of your continent. For My glory shall come in 10 years. Behold My servants, in these 10 years I shall need runners, fast runners; they that shall run to and fro in your nations. But where are those runners? For in a short while, the time will come. Therefore, raise runners for Me. Send them forth, and I shall bring the continent to a place it will shine.[1]

AT NATIONAL LEADERSHIP CONSULTATION IN LAGOS ON 26TH FEBRUARY, 2000

I declare I am the Lord. I ever existed. But My people I declare to you, who has believed My report? Have I not spoken to you in the past? I have declared that I desire your nation as a choice possession to make My Name known but your nation has not known Me.

Your Nation has not stretched out her hands to Me. I plead My case against your nation. I bring your nation to the place of a strong cry for there shall be a cry in your nation. These are the days I call you to Myself. Have I not declared? Do not be forgetful hearers. I plead My case against your nation so they will know me. Review what I have said to you. **I assure you, Nigeria will do My will and the nations shall rejoice as Nigeria does My will.** I will bring you to the place of acceptability they will have a pure language I will put My sickle into your land. I harvest the wicked for judgment. I harvest your nation. The ears that hear will tingle and My Cyrus shall come to lead your nation. Don't despair what will come. I have not left you without a witness. Look to Me for direction, says the Spirit of the Lord.[2]

AT ICCC CONFERENCE, SOUTH AFRICA

It dawned upon Gunnar Olson, founder of ICCC that it's time for the African nations to rise up and take their rightful place among the nations of the world. He made the following proclamations:

Africa, this is your Kairos moment, therefore arise and take your destiny.

Africa, be released and accept your divine mandate from heaven.

Africa, your shackles of slavery, poverty, limitations, idolatry, paganism, discrimination, exploitation, servitude, perversion, discord, witchcrafts, ancestral worship, Satanism, and all evil is crushed. Arise, Arise, Arise.

Africa, bring forth your sons and daughters who will arise and take their rightful place among the kings, princes, and nobles of the earth. Let them execute the righteousness of God, and advance the purposes of God to bring healing, prosperity, and manifestations of majesty, excellence, and glory.

Africa, the Lord will build a highway of holiness and righteousness, and everyone who walks on this highway will find refuge, strength and purpose.

Africa, all the nations of the earth will come marvel at your wisdom and glory.

Africa, Oh, Africa, the deepest fountains and resources of heaven that have been hidden deep in your belly because of the deeds of evil men, are now breaking forth because of the righteous remnants that have regarded the will of God higher than the opinions of men.

Africa, Arise, Arise, Arise. For the glory of God has risen upon you and your enemies are scattered.[3]

AT SOMA (SHARING OF MINISTRIES ABROAD) CONFERENCE 2000, SOUTH AFRICA

In summary the Lord promised He would change the face of Africa within a decade and that He would do bigger things than were done in the book of the Acts of the Apostles:

There was a time when this was called the Dark Continent; that time is over, says the Lord, because the light has shone upon you. The light of the Gospel is like a torch of fire that is being lit up by the Holy Spirit in this continent.

This continent will be known in the next ten years, as the continent that reversed the curse of the enemy—totally reversed the curse and started to walk in the path of blessing. The blessings will be shone forth to every nation in the world and professionals will look at Africa and will be totally amazed and will stand in awe saying, "what happened here? We cannot explain what happened to this continent. There was no possibility—there was no natural possibility whatsoever for this to happen." So everybody will say in this continent, "what happened here was not done by human hands, but by the Holy Spirit Himself."

There is an anointing for a miracle—an anointing for the supernatural upon this continent. There is a mantle upon this continent that is a miraculous mantle. It will fall upon anyone who will believe God, and literally capture the anointing and use it for the glory of the Lord. There are many, many conquests waiting for men and women, waiting to be conquerors. There are many challenges. There are many, many opportunities. This is the time and land of opportunity for the Kingdom of God.

There will be many, many Kingdom builders because of the anointing of the Holy Spirit. There are many, many men and women of God, who are waiting for a call from the Almighty—a supernatural kind of call—an anointing of the Holy Spirit. Now, there have been many, many great men of God who have risen up in the midst of calamity, and anguish, and sorrow, and have shaken fear out of their bodies, so to speak, and have traveled all over the world sowing the power of the Almighty God.

The Holy Spirit says, these men have not been unique. These men have been only the first fruits of what I want to do in Africa, says the Holy Spirit.

...I believe the times of miracles are coming to Africa in such a way that will literally overshadow the book of Acts. So many miracles and so powerful miracles that the shadow of men and women of God in this continent will heal the sick and raise the dead. It will happen so often that nobody will be amazed anymore when someone gets healed. The supernatural will be the natural thing in this continent . . . because the manifestations of the power of the Holy Spirit is growing, and growing, and growing, and growing higher in this continent. Africa will be an exporter of missionaries and prophecies.[4]

— HAROLD CABELLEROS, SOMA

MEETING, BEYOND AD2000, CAPE
TOWN SOUTH AFRICA, 2ND NOV, 2000

11

2002

PROPHECY BY CINDY JACOBS

The Lord says to Nigeria

I have given you a missionary spirit and am surely going to change the nations of the earth through you. But now I will give you the anointing to change your nation.

The Lord says, "I am going to begin to unravel the corrupt system in Nigeria and men will say it is impossible but I say with God all things are possible. There is going to be a revival in the Universities and this revival is going to be of such a large magnitude, that the revival in the Universities will affect the secondary schools and will affect the primary schools. And I am going to change Nigeria to the next generation" says God. And the Lord says "the unity of the leaders is coming. It's going to uproot and dethrone the occult. For I'm going to overthrow the occult spirit. And I'm going to use Nigeria to heal the rest of Africa because what happens in Nigeria will affect the whole continent."

The Lord says "I'm going to use the Nigerians in Russia. There will be many churches planted in Russia. The Lord says I'm going to use your nation. I'm going to use you in the Middle East." God says "I'm getting ready to change many things. I'm getting ready to expose this occult in the highest level. In the next few months, I'm going to tear it down and I'm going to make it shift and there will be a day violence will no longer be heard of in the streets of Nigeria. And it will be one of the safest nations on the face of the earth" says God. Hallelujah. God bless you and bless you.[1]

12

2005

AT PRETORIA, SOUTH AFRICA, MARCH
18, 2005

This is the fifth day of this holy convocation I called you from your nations to announce to you that the doors are opened. For years, ancient doors to the mystery of My grace have been locked to Africa. By the rebellion and disobedience of your fathers, the doors had been locked. By their idolatry, bloodshed and immorality, the doors had been locked. By deception, ignorance and foolishness, the doors have been locked. But today on this fifth day of your holy convocation, I the Lord God announce to you that the doors are opened! I have seen your tears. I have heard the cry of your heart. I have witnessed your willingness to repent. I have come to announce to you that the doors are opened to the mystery of Africa. The doors are opened to the mystery of your life. Open your eyes carefully and I will show you the doors within THE DOOR. As you walk into the door of the mystery of Africa, I will guide you into the mystery of your life. I, the Lord have come down to make announcement that the doors are open.

My celestial doors are open. Be careful to know the laws of the heavens. Be careful to use them to set My dominion on the earth. My terrestrial doors are open. I have come to shake the foundations of the earth. I have come to show you the mysteries of its wealth. Reach out your hands into the treasures of darkness. Reach out with My keys to unlock the hidden riches of secret places. The doors are opened to the thrones of Africa. I have come to harvest the souls of kings. This is the season of their harvest. I will loose the armour of kings and open to you the gates of their thrones.

The day has come for a continental gathering of kings at the feet of the King of kings. Open your eyes and you will see the multitudes of doors that are open to you, sons and daughters of Africa. I have opened doors to the marketplace. I have opened doors of witty inventions. I have opened the doors of knowledge and wisdom. I HAVE OPENED THE DOORS OF POWER. I have opened the doors of prophetic marriages. Did I not give you the keys to these doors? Did I not tell you how to open them? Yet now I have come down to open them Myself. I have released angels into your midst. They will unlock the ancient doors that have hindered My plans. They will break the bars of iron. They will cut them asunder. I have come to show Myself strong. The doors are open. Walk in and you will fulfill the mystery of My grace.[1]

13

2011

PROPHETIC WORD FROM PASTOR E.A. ADEBOYE AND PASTOR SAM ADEYEMI AS NARRATED BY GBENGA RICHMOND IN HIS BOOK, *GRINERIA: END OF THE OLD; BIRTH OF THE NEW*

In this 2012 book authored by Gbenga Richmond, he narrates some key events that occurred in 2011 and led to his belief in and strategic plans for a New Nigeria. He writes:

In August 2011, at the Holy Ghost convention that took place at the Redemption camp, along Lagos-Ibadan expressway, the General Overseer of the Redeemed Christian Church of God, (RCCG) Pastor E.A Adeboye said that God showed him a glimpse of what Nigeria will become in a few years and that what he saw was so beautiful that he would like to be alive to witness it. He also said God told him that He had raised a few men who would see to this transformation in no time.

In November 2011, by another stroke of destiny, I found myself in Lagos, saw a fanciful flyer lying around in a real estate office, picked it up only to discover the flyer was a publicity material by Daystar Christian Center were the Senior Pastor, Sam Adeyemi was to play host to guest speakers in what turned out to be an earth-shaking leadership conference titled, "Excellence in Leadership Conference 2011," with the theme: Innovate ... Change your world.

The convener of the conference, Pastor Sam Adeyemi, said that God is raising a new generation of leaders in Nigeria-called the 'take over' generation—who the powers of darkness cannot threaten, overwhelm or dominate—to replace the present crop of leaders in government.

He said though the new leaders God is raising may be lost in obscurity physically now; they will eventually fulfill purpose because they have the spiritual capacity bestowed on them by God for excellence in leadership.

He said the devil is currently distracting a special category of Nigerians with a special kind of poverty because he knows that if they come into wealth, they will become special change agents that will bring untold wealth to this nation.

He said God told him that He is anointing [1]"Davids"…

14

2014

PROPHECY BY PASTOR DEBO ADESINA OF *THE WATERGATE CHURCH, OTA* ON NOVEMBER 23, 2014; 4:47AM

Nigeria shall praise the name of the Lord. Even though, we seem to be plunged into darkness, however, with the eyes and ears that see and hear the invisible and the inaudible . . . I SEE AND HEAR SUNRISE, SUNRISE, SUNRISE IS COMING OVER NIGERIA. Selah.[1]

15

2015

PROPHETIC WORD FOR NEW NIGERIA BY DR. JONATHAN DAVID AT THE GLOBAL LEADERS SUMMIT 2015 (PART 1)

Dr. Jonathan David is the Founder and Senior Pastor of All Nations Sanctuary (formerly Full Gospel Centre) Muar, a governing kingdom church in Muar, Johor, Malaysia. He is also the Presiding Apostle of the International Strategic Alliance of Apostolic Churches (ISAAC), a network of governing churches and ministers across the nations. He gave the following 2-part prophecy at the Global Leaders Summit of 2015.

God shows me that Nigeria will be in a special place. Nigeria will become the bread basket for the

North. God will begin to touch the land. I can see the Holy Spirit touching the land of Nigeria causing it to become fertile. Out of the ground will come forth the gold. Out of the ground will come forth the silver. Out of the ground will come forth resources. And the North will be irrigated by what God is doing and thus become the food basket providing resources. They will begin to replenish and their money will change nations. Their money will rebuild cities with the resources that they have [and] with the people that they have. God will begin to use them as a model nation moving them out of corruption into righteousness. Moving them from a place of poverty to a place of wealth. Moving them back onto the ladders of promotion because righteousness will strike at the heart of every corruption and the work of the enemy is going to cease.

I see Nigeria rising in a fresh new way. This is a new day in Nigeria. This is a new day, a new hour. No more turning back. It's not just one term; God is going to extend the term. He is going to push it again and again. Again and again, righteousness will be the order of the day. I say again and again, righteousness will be the order of the day. The one coming after President Buhari is taking the presidency to the next level and the next one coming in and the next one coming in . . . God is going to give four or five terms to Nigeria so that Nigeria will completely turn around — not just for this president alone. There will be four or five more and they will continue to bring reformation and transformation upon the earth.

Nigeria will not just rise for a short moment like a shooting star and then disappear out of context. God is saying 'I'm going to build an enduring house in Nigeria.' He is going to remove the powers of death. Corruption and corrupt men shall no longer walk on the soil. God touched the soil; he says it's fertile. He touched the soil and say it is holy because He is coming down by the power of the Spirit. He is going to bring about new change because he is going to give hope back to Nigeria. He is going to give back hope to Africa. If Nigeria can change, all of Africa can change. And God is saying this is the message I'm going to send — 'I'm going to send the message all across Africa and turn things around in a powerful way.'

So get ready, a new day is born! A new day is being birthed. Corruption is removed; corrupt men are removed; the things of negative influence have been removed. God will begin to sow righteousness. Break up the fallow ground.

I see that they will rise in Agriculture in a very powerful way. The people will not be poor any more. The ground will make them rich. The ground in Nigeria will become fruitful. We speak to the ground in Nigeria, "Let oil come forth! Let minerals come forth! Let life food come forth! Let all other sorts of blessings come forth from the ground!" And God will begin to bless the land because He's redeemed the land in a powerful way.

Nigeria, you shall be great again! Nigeria, you shall be strong again! This is our word to you in the name of Jesus. Every Nigerian will hear the sound of this prophecy and begin to take courage. It's not by race that we win — it's not the North winning; it's not the South winning; It's not the South-West winning. God is in control. He wants everyone to be a champion. He wants everyone to be a leader . . . so that the nation can be filled with the resources of heaven and reformation that will take place. Transformation will take place. [Nigeria] will become a model nation in the next four or five terms that is ahead in the presidency.

New things are going to happen. Men that create strife will no longer be around because God will judge them and remove the power. He will judge them and remove their influence so

that the new generation that is rising will not look for corrupt men — they are not going to look for recycled leadership material because they are going to lead. There is a whole wave of new things that's going to happen. The young men in Nigeria are going to rise. There is going to be a whole crop of people rising in Nigeria — the young men and young women — those who are professionals, those who think professionally, those who think about progress, those who think about the things that God is saying. They will arise. They will arise and do a powerful work. They will begin to speak in every corner, in every place, in every domain — a new generation of young men and young women will come up.

Nigeria, you will be saved! Nigeria will be clothed in glory! The days of your shame is gone. The days of your reproach is gone because God is not only going to give you one president, He is going to give you three or four more terms into the future so that the nation will turn around completely. Your currency will become strong. God is going to use the powerful work of the Spirit in the nation and begin to cause infrastructures and designs so that the currency will become stronger and stronger. The money in Nigeria will go everywhere. It will start rebuilding nations — not only in the nation but in the nations round about. Supernatural things will happen. Amen.

We bless Nigeria, we say you shall never be the same again. We say no more turning back. There is no more reverse gear for Nigeria. You shall rise and go forward. You shall rise and run to the frontline. You shall rise and break forth. In your rising, many other nations will begin to rise.

Africa hear; hear what the Lord is doing in Nigeria. Africa, hear the sound of His voice. Africa, hear the sounds of reform. Africa., start to hear what God is doing in the midst of you. He is beginning to shake the nations so strong and mighty and bring a nation down to His feet so that they will worship Him as King of kings and Lord of lords. He's not the God of the North; He's not the God of the South; He's the God Almighty! He is God of the nations. Nigeria, receive your King! Nigeria, receive your Lord! Receive your Master! Receive your Saviour! The nation will open up in the name of Jesus. We bless you, Nigeria. We will never be the same again! You will not return to your old ways. You will not return to the ways of corruption and darkness and all kinds of violence. You shall go forth in the power of the Holy Ghost. The hand of the Lord shall be mighty upon you to make your nation safe and strong and mighty and God will clothe you with all kinds of resources and your cities will be filled with people who are happy and glad — who know that God is their Lord. Halleluyah! Be blessed! See the manifestation![1]

PROPHETIC WORD FOR NEW NIGERIA BY DR. JONATHAN DAVID AT THE GLOBAL LEADERS SUMMIT 2015 (PART 2)

...God is saying, Nigeria, the days of your violence is over. We speak to all the violent groups across Nigeria — in the North — we speak to you in the Name of Jesus that you put down your weapons of war. Stop causing confusion and chaos from the North or in the South. God is arresting violence. In this time that God is going to raise up His own president — His own men — He's going to crash the head of the enemy and begin to push it all the way out of the territory. Violence will not be heard in your boundary. God is going to cause them to scatter. He's going to cause violence to scatter from your land. There will be no disruption of families. There will be no destruction of women and children.

God is saying He's bringing about deliverance in Nigeria — that he's going to cause Nigeria to become like the bright shining star. When it happens in Nigeria, it will happen in other parts of the land. Africa will turn around because Nigeria has changed.

God is saying it is time for you to allow His plans and purpose for Nigeria to come in. The spirit of violence be bound! The shedding of innocent blood be bound. God is saying that each men will serve his own God. There is no reason for the South to look at the North in fear; no reason for the North to look to the South in anger. God is saying that he will give to each one their own portion. You can call on the name of your God and live in peace and we will call on the name of our God and live in peace because God is saying that He's going to cause supernatural things to happen and He's going to cause the dismantling of violence so that the nation is going to become free . . . You shall not be divided any more. The Lord says the dividing line is over — it's not about the North, South or South-West — God is saying to Nigeria, "You are a new Nigeria!" You are not divided; you shall be one people. And God is making this decision for you. God is overriding and overruling all the decisions of wicked men so that evil will stop. Nigeria, be blessed...

You are not going to look to the days of the past; God is going to birth a New Nigeria. Get ready for the breaking forth of a new dawn. We proclaim to you, Nigeria, the breaking of a new dawn! The dawn of peace. The dawn of God's blessings and exponential grace. We from the nations of the world speak to you in Jesus' name. Be at peace. Be in prosperity. Be in the supernatural blessing of God. Even the diaspora of Nigeria right across the nations of the world — many will return back to Nigeria and they will begin to see that when they return, the house of God is filled with bread and all the provision they needed. They will say 'Let's go back to the place of our inheritance.' And many sons and daughters will come from afar and they will help rebuild the ancient ruins so Nigeria will never be the same again. They will never be brought into reproach again because the Lord God is set His face upon you so that Nigeria will be saved. Nigeria will be blessed. Nigeria will show the way. They will say "If it happened in Nigeria, it can happen in any part of the continent." It is true. It shall begin to break out all across Africa. There will be changes that will be taking place in the high places in governments so that the people in each nation will begin to have hope in their hearts. Hope will be given back to Africa. You will be like the city — 'The Cape of Good Hope.'

The Lord is saying this shall become your portion. Be blessed! We bless you from the nations of the world. We say Nigeria, come into your New Day! The breaking of a new dawn. The day of God's blessing and peace — without violence or pestilence, without all kinds of sickness and oppression. The nation, be blessed! And you will rise! Halleluyah![2]

2016

PROPHETIC SERMON PREACHED BY PASTOR OLUBI JOHNSON OF SCRIPTURE PASTURE CHRISTIAN CENTRE

The following is the transcript of a prophetic sermon preached by Pastor Olubi Johnson of Scripture Pasture Christian Centre, Ibadan, Nigeria on January 4, 2016. It is titled *Building Up Zion From Beyond The Rivers of Ethiopia*. I believe it is very instructive for the prophetic destiny of Nigeria.

2016 has been declared to be a year of Jubilee during which there will be a manifestation of the glory of God by the power of the Spirit without measure which has been released (at the synchronization of the blood moon and feast of

Tabernacles in September 2015) but not yet manifested (like it was with the Lord Jesus at **John's baptism (Jn.1.31-33) but manifested at Cana (Jn.2.11)**.

For the glory to be made manifest, Zion must be built up to a threshold level by the Word and the power of the Spirit without measure that has been released BUT NOT manifested:

Psalms 102:13 KJV: Thou shalt **arise,** *and* **have mercy upon Zion: for the time to favour her, yea, the set time, is come.**

Psalms 102:16 KJV: **When the LORD shall build up Zion, he shall appear in his glory.**

Acts 20:32 KJV: And now, brethren, I commend you to God, and to **the word of his grace, which is able to build you up, and to give you an inheritance** among all them, which are sanctified.

Observe that the purpose of the building up is to give us an inheritance: the manifestation of the power of the Spirit without measure.

Jude 1:20 KJV: But you, beloved, **build yourselves up** [*founded*] on your most holy faith [*make progress, rise like an edifice higher and higher*]**, praying in the Holy Spirit;**

As we write this, building up has started and is being pioneered from beyond the rivers of Ethiopia in the land the rivers divide: Nigeria according to the prophetic scriptures:

Isaiah 18:1-2 NKJV: Woe to **the land** shadowed with buzzing wings, **which *is* beyond the rivers of Ethiopia,** (2) Which sends ambassadors by sea, Even in vessels of reed on the waters, *saying,* "Go, swift messengers, to **a nation tall and smooth *of skin,*** To a people terrible from their beginning onward, A nation powerful and treading down, **whose land the rivers divide."**

Isaiah 18:7 NKJV: In that time **a present will be brought to the LORD of hosts from a people tall and smooth *of skin,*** And from a people terrible from their beginning onward, **a nation powerful and treading down, Whose land the rivers divide— To the place of the name of the LORD of hosts, To Mount Zion.**

These scriptures speak prophetically of a spiritual people: tall and of smooth skin—symbolically speaking of great spiritual stature and smooth or pure character that will be living in a physical nation beyond the rivers of Ethiopia that will be divided by rivers.

We can see the 'tall stature' and 'smooth skin' symbolizing the perfect church in

Ephesians 4:12-13 KJV: For **the perfecting of the saints**, for the work of the ministry, for the edifying of the body of Christ: (13) Till we all come in the unity of the faith, and of the knowledge of the Son of God, unto a perfect man, **unto the measure of the stature of the fulness of Christ:**

Ephesians 5:27 KJV: That he might present it to himself **a glorious church, not having spot, or wrinkle, or any such thing; but that it should be holy and without blemish.**

Also, we can see that this church will be a powerful, militant church that will overcome all its enemies this is shown symbolically in

Joel 2:2-3 NKJV: A day of darkness and gloominess, A day of clouds and thick darkness, Like the morning *clouds* spread over the mountains. **A people** *come,* **great and strong, the like of whom has never been; Nor will there ever be any** *such* **after them,** Even for many successive generations. (3) A fire devours before them, And behind them a flame burns; The land *is* like the Garden of Eden before them, And behind them a desolate wilderness; **Surely nothing shall escape them.**

Only Nigeria and the church of Jesus Christ in her that is growing into the perfection and fulness of Christ: spiritual Zion fits this unique prophetic description.

The rivers Niger and Benue divide Nigeria.

The church in Nigeria that is growing into the perfection and fulness of Christ is symbolically called Zion and spiritual Israel—the seed of Abraham through the Lord Jesus:

Psalms 50:2 NKJV: Out of **Zion, the perfection of beauty**, God will shine forth.

Galatians 3:29 AMP: And **if you belong to Christ** [*are in Him Who is Abraham's Seed*], **then you are Abraham's offspring** and [*spiritual*] heirs according to promise.

Why is the pioneering from beyond the rivers of Ethiopia?

It is instructive to note that the perfect church will not be in Nigeria alone: it will just be pioneered in Nigeria and then spread to all nations. This is similar to the fact **the birth of the church was** pioneered in Israel and later spread to all nations (Acts 1:8); and the reformation of the church was pioneered in Germany in 1517 by Martin Luther and later spread to all nations.

The purposes of God in the **3 prophetic days (3 1000-year periods according to 2 Peter 3:8) of the church** were pioneered and now are being pioneered by the descendants of the 3 sons of Noah: **Shem, Japheth and Ham (Genesis 10:1).**

1. The birth of the church in Jerusalem by Israel (the sons of Shem).

2. The reformation of the Church in Germany by Martin Luther (the sons of Japheth).

3. The perfection of the Church in Nigeria (the sons of Ham).

We see the characteristics of this perfect church in:

Zephaniah 3:10-14 NKJV: From beyond the rivers of Ethiopia My worshipers, the daughter of My dispersed ones, shall bring My offering. (11) In that day you shall not be shamed for any of your deeds in which you transgress against Me; For then I will take away from your midst those who rejoice in your pride, And **you**

shall no longer be haughty in My holy mountain. (12) I will leave in your midst A meek and humble people, and they shall trust in the Name of the LORD. (13) The remnant of Israel shall do no unrighteousness and speak no lies, nor shall a deceitful tongue be found in their mouth; for they shall feed *their* flocks and lie down, and no one shall make *them* afraid." (14) Sing, O daughter of Zion! Shout, O Israel! Be glad and rejoice with all *your* heart, O daughter of Jerusalem!

The 3 major characteristics are:

1. A meek and lowly heart (verse 12): giving access to great grace and wisdom (1 Peter 5:5 and Proverbs 11:2).
2. Tongue tamed (no lies or deceit—verse 13) by the power of Holy Spirit so enabling perfection (James 3:2).
3. No fear (none shall make them afraid—verse 13) because perfect love casteth out fear (1 John 4:18).

So, as we continue to build up ourselves by the blood (Hebrews 13:20-21), Word (1 John 2:5) and the Spirit (1 John 4:12-13) with a meek and lowly heart, so taming the tongue and perfecting the love of God, the glory of God will soon be manifest![1]

A REVELATION GIVEN TO OPE ADEJUYIGBE IN 2016

I saw the train of Nigeria running faster than the plane of the Queen of England. I wanted to be part of that future as I continued to question how a train would outrun an airplane but I was told to stay in England and help translate/interpret. I have since then believed without a doubt, that Nigeria will enjoy supernatural speed once "the train" begins to move. Some days ago before the protests (in October 2020) began, I woke up with this statement from scripture said to me in my sleep: "I Daniel understood by the books…" As I continued to meditate on that, I became aware that the acceleration of the train would begin between Nigeria's 60th and 70th Independence anniversary. It will be a decade of recovery. I heard 'acceleration' — that the rebuilding will happen like Jerusalem and the walls — that Nigerians in diaspora are like Daniels, Nehemiahs and Ezras are like the exiled that will play a part.[2]

17

2017

A REVELATION RECEIVED BY DR JOSEPH OLOWE, PRESIDING SERVANT, KINGDOM DOMINION MINISTRIES INTERNATIONAL, USA

Below is an excerpt from *"Vision 2030: The Rebirth of Nigeria"* based on a revelation shown to Dr Joseph Olowe a Nigerian-American in 2017. He published the prophecy and a proposed action plan as *Vision 2030: The Rebirth of Nigeria — From Independence to Spiritual Deliverance, Rebirthing and Liberty (1960 - 2030).*

God has designated Nigeria as His place of habitation. He is delighted in us as a nation and thus, He is ready to rise and deliver Nigeria from the corruption that has robbed her of her destined glory. God delights in people, in the multitude of people is the king's honour, so it is not a coincidence that Nigeria is the most populous nation in Africa and arguably with the most vibrant expression of heavenly inclined Christianity.

God is about to do a new thing in Nigeria, no doubt, however, He will never do anything outside the purview of His Word. Thus, He brought the Word unto me—just as He did to Daniel (Daniel 9:2)—in an open revelation, on the 19th of May, 2017.

THE VISION

The Lord spoke to me in mid-air on my way to Nigeria. It was in a British Airways Flight 74 between Heathrow and Murtala Mohammed Airport. He declared **"VISION 2030"** for Nigeria and shed some light on the future of the nation. In this incredible revelation, I asked the Lord to give me an assurance that this nation called Nigeria can be redeemed. He answered clearly and audibly from His Word—Isaiah 66:8. He said it will be said of Nigeria:

"Who has heard such a thing? Who has seen such a thing?" Shall the earth be made to bring forth in ONE DAY? Or shall A NATION be born at once?

The Lord said to me from this verse, that He desires the cooperation of HIS PEOPLE. He desires that Zion (the church) will arise and address the corruption and compromise within her borders, and by so doing, be empowered to address the same across the nation. Then shall Zion travail in prayers, and a new Nigeria shall come forth.

If my people will not rise up to pray, Nigeria may not go beyond SEVENTY YEARS or by reason of strength and providence, EIGHTY YEARS. She may become a divided nation and that is not my will for her. I have reserved her as a BATTLE AXE in the warfare for the evangelisation of the entire universe. Yes, behold, my plans and purposes for Nigeria is great.[1] It is for this reason that I have chosen certain groups of people and called their entire generation to lead this end time harvest. As the time approaches, I will begin to reveal and make known the remnant that will the lead this assignment. First, however, Nigeria must be able to make it past 2030, so that my hand upon the nation can be revealed.

I say it again that I will make Nigeria into the envy of many developed nations of the world, because I, the Lord, will punish them for their neglect and non-committal attitude to this nation.[2] I alone will deliver her and will share My glory with no graven image.

Let my **DANIELS** across the nation—as many as are willing to abandon their own interests in ministry—come together to **BRING FORTH THEIR STRONG REASONS** and I will heal the land. And I will do with all the people that have destroyed this nation as I have done to all the kings that stood in my way. Ask Bashan, Og, Nebuchadnezzar, Pharaoh and many more.

"Produce your cause, saith the Lord; bring forth your strong reasons, saith the King of Jacob. Let them bring them forth, and shew us what shall happen: let them shew the former things, what they be, that we may consider them, and know the latter end of them; or declare us things for to come. Shew the things that are to come hereafter, that we may know that ye are gods: yea, do good, or do evil, that we may be dismayed, and behold it together."

— ISAIAH 41:21-23

Nigeria is likened to the ship heading for Tarshish with Jonah onboard. Every Jonah at every level in the society that has refused to do as I have commanded them and thus bringing much loss to My people, I, the Lord, will loot their treasury and do with with them as I have done to the house of Ahab. My Jehus have been appointed and will stop at nothing until the total destruction of all the designated Jonahs whom I have appointed to heal the land but have chosen to do otherwise.

Thus says the Lord, I will begin to push some of them overboard this ship called Nigeria, and my designated whales of affliction will begin to tear them in pieces, until they repent and confess—or perish. **I, the Lord, will arise with vengeance in defence of my beloved nation. This will be the first sign: I will cause major confusion in all the major political parties, thereby revealing the heart of the wicked people behind the sudden rise of terrorism.**[3]

18

2020

PROPHECY CONCERNING NIGERIA GIVEN BY PASTOR DEBO ADESINA AT ABEOKUTA BELIEVERS MEETING (ABM), A PRAYER MEETING HELD VIA ZOOM ON MONDAY, JULY 27, 2020 BY 10PM

I believe strongly that we are coming into a season in which justice will be seen in our nation.

We are coming into a season where there will be judgment across the land.

We are coming into a season in which some of the things that have been hidden are going to be exposed.

We are coming into a season in which people that

have walked deceptively, but who we think are doing the right things, will be exposed.

[In this season], those we do not know are involved in practices that are very shady will be exposed.

Nigeria will not sink but will rise!

We are coming into a season in which we will see a strong justice in the land.

What I see is like seeing the leg of a man, which I perceive is more like a feet — let me use the word 'feet' of a man — which is the Feet of the Lord walking through the land, walking through the land, walking through the land and He is going to establish justice in our nation.

That is going to happen in the days to come. This is what I perceive the Spirit of the Lord saying. Amen.[1]

PROPHECY BY REVEREND TOKUNBO ADEJUWON, NATIONAL DIRECTOR, RHEMA BIBLE TRAINING CENTER NIGERIA, ON SEPTEMBER 19, 2020 AT RHEMA CONFERENCE

We are in the shallow waters of another new beginning.

We are in the shallow waters of another new beginning

We are in the shallow waters of another new beginning

A new beginning in our nation

In our nation, a new beginning

A turning point

Some changes will happen

And it will be the hand of the Lord

That brought them to pass

And we'll all say,

"This only could have been God."[2]

A PROPHETIC PRAYER BY BRO GBILE AKANNI OF PEACE HOUSE, GBOKO, NIGERIA.

The following prayer was published as an animated video on the Facebook page of Peace House, Gboko on October 1, 2020. It was not specified at what event or when the prayer was originally recorded but the words thereof are a good way to end this collection of prophecies.

Nigeria is not too difficult for God to change and I stand here to prophesy that Nigeria will not continue like this. Vagabonds and Esaus will not eat Nigeria completely. God has a prophetic destiny for this nation, and let all men hear me: You cannot kick for long against the pricks. The eye of the Lord is upon this nation. He has invested so much in this country. Exploiters, raiders — those who just thought that this is the place to occupy — [know that] the Lion of Judah is in our midst.

Let it be known to all men that He Who planted this nation has not abandoned it. The Minister of State and several of Your children that have benefitted from the ministry of Scripture Union many years ago — [those] whom by Your mercy

You are bringing up — how I plead with you on their behalf that strength will come into their spirits. Strength to stand for God. Strength never to bow. [Like] the three sons of Hebrew who said they will rather burn than bow, and by their lives — not by the majority — they brought Babylon on their knees. Therefore, Lord, I pray that Your servants who are standing out there, empower them in the Name of Jesus! Let faith rise in their spirits, knowing that Your people — Your church — is praying and crying to You that Nigeria is going to have a transformation.

Everything look contrary but we know our God. We know the Lion of the Tribe of Judah. [Though] people say "it cannot be done", but we saw You doing it before.

Egypt took over the people of Israel for 430 years. They made them slaves. They treated them as if they will become nothing. But when it was time — when You heard their cry — nobody has ever thought that a bondage of 430 years can be reversed in less than two months. You did it in one night! One night! And I'm asking you, O God, when you turn the captivity of Nigeria around, we will be as men who are just dreaming. You will put a song of victory [in our mouths]. Nigeria will praise the Lord! Righteousness will return to Nigeria. Governance that fears God will return to Nigeria.

In our schools, in our universities, educational curriculum — everywhere the fear of God had been tampered with, we command it to return in the name of Jesus!

Thank You for hearing us. Thank You for You will do more than we can ask or imagine. Blessed be Your Name. In Jesus Christ's name, we have prayed. Amen.[3]

PROPHECY BY PROPHET SADHU SUNDAR SELVARAJ

This huge Angel over Nigeria reveals;

There is going to come a new beginning for this Nation Nigeria. A change is coming in the political arena of this country — that which many people are not expecting. A sudden change will come quickly…

Many political leaders will be changed. The unrighteous ones will be removed from office. God's righteous men will be voted even to the highest office. Many governors of the nation will be changed and true righteous ones who carry the sword of the Lord in their hands will be stationed in this nation. Even in the provincial areas, in the cities . . . political changes are coming, and it is for righteousness sake.

Let the children arise and put on strength. The army of children will arise and put on much strength like never before. And they shall march as a single unit army to pull down and destroy the works of the devil. And let her youth arise and put on the armour like a strong marching force of power — of soldiers putting on strength, putting on the whole armour of God from the head to the toe and strengthened with might from on high.

God will root out evil from the churches. Every false church, every false pastor, every false prophet will be rooted out of this nation and will be cast into the sea of Abyss, never to be found and never to be known again. Let the true righteous ones arise! Let the true righteous people of God arise! Let the Land be cleansed of its evil. Let the land that has seen violence be now put away so that righteousness will come forth from the Land.

An upheaval and a change is coming to this nation that will affect the political, economical and spiritual areas of this nation. The church will undergo great changes and transformation. The Lord has willed it and the angels of God will effect the will of God by causing and forcing changes to come in the churches.[4]

O God of creation,
Direct our noble cause;
Guide our Leaders right:
Help our Youth the truth to know,
In love and honesty to grow,
And living just and true,
Great lofty heights attain,
To build a nation where peace and justice reign.

PA S.G. ELTON: A TRIBUTE

AYODEJI ABODUNDE

The following tribute to Late Pa Sydney Elton is an excerpt from Ayodeji Abodunde's introduction into a beautiful and comprehensive highly-recommended biographical work on the life, ministry and theology of this apostolic figure in the history of the Nigerian church — *Messenger: Sydney Elton and the Making of Pentecostalism in Nigeria.*

Indeed one would be hard pressed to find a preacher who took the designation "missionary to Nigeria" more seriously than Elton did. Although Elton came to Nigeria as just one more missionary of the Apostolic Church with headquarters in Penygroes, Wales, he soon came to believe, to really believe, that he had been *sent* to Nigeria, so much so that if he had not come on the platform of the Apostolic Church, he would still have come, that he would not have been sent to any other place but Nigeria, because he had an assignment to fulfil—a divine assignment, divinely packaged for the nation called Nigeria. Elton was so conscious of his role as God's messenger to Nigeria that a casual observer could not be blamed for judging it to be extreme or bordering on self-aggrandisement.

Elton considered himself a messenger who had been sent to a nation destined to play a crucial role in God's end-time plan. He approached this assignment with an almost extreme sense of responsibility, working as if any failure on his part had the potential to jeopardize God's intention for the nation. He saw himself and his mission as enormously crucial to the spiritual destiny of Nigeria. This created in him an emotional attachment to the country; indeed, it is clear he had psychologically shed his British citizenship at some point. He declared in 1982, "I want to warn you, and serve you notice, that I'm going to have my interest in Nigeria, whether you like it or not. I may be a white man, but this is where my inheritance is. God has ... brought me to Nigeria, and I've been here these forty-five years, and nobody will take me back to a place where I've got nothing. This is where I've got it all. Here! And there are ten thousand people already in heaven, because I'm here and there's another ten thousand waiting to go with me. Yes, my inheritance is here and more than that, I've put my feet in enough soil in Nigeria for me to say, that's mine, that's mine!" This grave sense of mission, expressed in different hues throughout his career, underlies everything he did, and it is only from this perspective that we can truly understand and appreciate his ministry of half a century in the country.

For fifty years, Elton continuously challenged a nation by his radical spiritual outlook. In the 1950s, he spearheaded on a national scale the first wave of modern-day mass revivals in the country. In the 1960s he provided the platform for some of the leading figures in the global Pentecostal movement to have a major influence on the direction of Nigeria's Christianity. Beginning in the late 1960s, he embarked on an ambitious project of training the next generation; he sought them out wherever they could be found, especially in universities and colleges, and encouraged them with every resource at his disposal to lay hold of their destiny in God. He envisioned a spiritual army of young Nigerian Christians boldly marching through the nation establishing God's government everywhere they went. Battling not a few conservative forces on his way, he stopped at nothing to ensure that a generation clearly understood its place in God's plan and had the courage to pursue it. This resulted in a massive spiritual shift that defined Christianity among young people in the sixties, seventies and eighties, and directly led to the emergence of the charismatic movement in Nigeria.

Elton's emphasis on the importance of the power and the gifts of the Holy Spirit to the present-day ministry of the church was perhaps the single most important factor in the emergence of the charismatic movement in Nigeria. Elton pioneered systematic teaching on the operation of the gifts of the Spirit and the practical application of these gifts in the lives of Christians in Nigeria through his seminars on the subject on university campuses, through one-on-one and small group meetings at his base in Ilesa, and through teaching on the subject in churches and conferences around the country. Virtually all the Christian leaders who were influenced by Elton agree that one of the greatest legacies he bequeathed to their generation, and by extension to the nation, was laying the foundation of their understanding and practical application of the gifts of the Holy Spirit

—both by teaching and impartation. This legacy played a significant role in equipping a generation of Nigerian youth for the Christian ministry as church leaders, missionaries, Christian educators, and Christian workers in all spheres of spiritual endeavour.

When Pentecostalism was still struggling to be recognized as a valid tradition in Nigeria's Christianity, Elton had seen its emergence on the global stage and called on Nigerian Pentecostals to prepare to take the gospel to the ends of the earth. He unrelentingly prophesied that Pentecostal Christianity in Nigeria would lead a spiritual revival in Africa and the Western nations that would usher the church worldwide into the glory that has been reserved for the last days. To borrow a phrase from historian Ron Chernow, Elton was "the messenger from a future that we now inhabit."

Perhaps Elton's greatest legacy to Nigerian Christianity was the vision he cast for the future. He spent the last ten years of his life articulating what the church would look like at the end of the age. He believed the church at the close of the age would be so radically different in outlook than what obtained in his day, and that only a courageous generation would dare to make a transition to this new and final phase of God's programme. Elton saw a daring generation of Nigerian and African Christians who in the last days would lead global Christian thought and experience. Elton believed he was called to prepare the way for that generation, that he was called to point the way to the future.

Elton carried the DNA of a warrior: a spartan life, a courageous spirit, a fierce devotion. He dared to go to new places in the Spirit, even when no one else would follow. He was a frontiersman, always feeling for what might lie ahead, always reaching for what had yet been unexplored, always thirsting for what God might still have in stock. Figuratively speaking, Elton lived in tents throughout his life, ever ready to move at the first scent of a new move of the Holy Spirit. . . .

By the time Elton died in 1987, his ministry and collaborations had completely reshaped Nigeria's spiritual landscape.[1]

A CALL TO ORDER

DR TONY RAPU

The following piece was written by Dr Tony Rapu in 2002 and serves as an apt introduction to the rest of this collection of Prophecies concerning Nigeria. It was featured in Political Spiritualities: The Pentecostal Revolution in Nigeria *written by Ruth Marshall.*[1]

A report recently circulated in the United States intelligence community predicting that Nigeria may become a failed state in the next fifteen years is currently making waves among Nigerians. The document cited incidents of ethnic unrest and political bickering and concluded that Nigeria could very likely break up in a civil conflagration. Not surprisingly both the presidency and the National Assembly condemned the reports. Our House of Representatives has directed that

Nigeria's own intelligence agency investigate the reliability of the report. . . . The amusing side of the story is that we scarcely need a foreign intelligence body to convince us that this nation is potentially headed for ruin. Every social index points to just such a future. Nigerians already live in the midst of a general infrastructural collapse and grinding poverty. We are told that 70% of the country's population lives on below $1 a day. Less than half the population has access to safe drinking water. Life expectancy in Nigeria is now 49 years. The unmitigated failure of NEPA means that production costs are outrageously high. This and other factors have brought the manufacturing sector into a virtually comatose state. The educational sector is in crisis, despoiled by frequent strikes, student uprisings and violent campus cult clashes. The Central Bank of Nigeria recently disclosed that there are at least 6 million unemployed graduates currently floating around the labour market; as much for their own lack of skills as the general lack of jobs. HIV/AIDS is decimating a significant segment of the population with latest estimates placing the number of those living with the plague at one in five. The country is ranked among the bottom ten in the global human development index. Our economy has been decimated by official theft. Religious and ethnic violence still tend to break out sporadically claiming thousands of lives. . . .

There are two ways of looking at the situation we have found ourselves in. By far the easier would be to digest the information with its gory details and conclude that the end is near; that the wholesale disintegration of the Nigerian state predicted by the American intelligence analysts is inevitable and simply resign ourselves to fate. Or we can look at the seemingly insurmountable decay that surrounds us and hear within the apocalyptic tone of statistics and foreign intelligence reports a call to action. But this call is not to the institution of civil government as we know it, for that has already been weighed on the scales and found wanting. This call to arms is to the Church as the authentic custodian of the Nation's destiny to take responsibility for Nigeria. The Divine blueprint for National redemption and subsequent transformation begins with a familiar clarion call *"If My people who are called by My Name . . ."* If the people of God will act purposefully, God Himself will heal the land. In practical terms this means that we must begin to understand that the redemption of Nations is tied to the purpose of the Church. But that is only as far as the Church recognizes that its mandate in the preaching of the gospel of the kingdom includes the concept of National transformation and societal reform. . . . It is only the principles of this "government," principles for an ordered society; Christian principles which many of the developed nations themselves have successfully applied that will bring reform to our land or any other land. Unfortunately many Christians are under the unscriptural impression that there is a division between the sacred and the secular. We have adopted a "church-building" mentality and have conceded the world to unruly and incompetent men. Some declare that religion and politics do not mix. They are gravely mistaken because society implicitly recognizes that all civil authority derives validity from a higher authority—God. A new consciousness of righteousness and morality is needed. A re-orientation movement where the values of the dignity of labor, discipline and orderliness would reign is a great necessity. The driving force for National Transformation will be those people who understand that only the introduction of the Divine into this complex national equation can bring a resolution.

Some of these leaders as they begin to reign as kings over their local empires, now begin to exercise rulership over the church and the people in it. . . . Very gradually a grotesque monster of control and intimidation may appear behind the concept of unity and vision. Personal liberty and the giftings of the people are then destroyed as they are brought into bondage of a man-centered organization. God warned Israel against the dangers of a man-king. . . . This is true today in that you'll find people weary, tired and burnt but serving the will of their organization yet having no intimacy with the God they claim to serve. . . . The people end up being enslaved to the vision of the king. Kings must live in comfort. Kings need money to increase the size of their empires, and unfortunately the people always have to pay for the personal ambition of the king. Those who help the king extend his empire are handsomely rewarded. And those who express concern over the king's strategies may be sidelined. Even those who started well may become ensnared in the trappings of power. . . . The lure of money, power, influence, position and a desire to be relevant in the lives of other people contributes to the creation of this monster on the pulpit. . . . The leader is trapped, the people themselves are trapped, everyone knows there is a problem but no one knows what to do. Currently, there is a raging battle in the church and the contention is between the truth and a lie being presented as the truth. . . . Unfortunately, many are caught in a strong delusion and believe this perversion of truth. Many sincere and faithful believers find themselves living and endorsing a lie.

Christianity is the description of prophetic life on planet earth. It is not a religion, it is not a faith, it is a lifestyle! Today Christianity is a confused term. We have people who have no idea what God is saying, calling themselves Christians. There are some activities attributable to us that are not of God, but we have just done them over time and they have basically become bondage—a stronghold that exists inside our minds. Probably, it was some printer who bound the book that first called it the Holy Bible. The printed pages in themselves are not holy, it is the Spirit and the principles of the Word, operating in the lives of those who believe which confer holiness. The true Church has no religion, what we have is a life style. It is very important we know that it is not only about something we believe, but about who we become, for the pattern of the Word is to re-incarnate itself in the lives of men. In this way the Word becomes flesh and dwells within us. This Christianity is a lifestyle that we should function in, in all dimensions of life. When we understand this in our hearts and not only in our heads, it helps us to transform what we are and how we function and operate. We don't go to church! We are the Church![2]

SAVING NIGERIA

PASTOR OLUBI JOHNSON

The following piece was written by Pastor Olubi Johnson in March 2013. It is similar to the prophetic sermon featured in the chapter titled "2016" but with more content on *how* God will save Nigeria.

- **Isaiah 18:1-2 NKJV:** Woe to **the land** shadowed with buzzing wings, **Which *is* beyond the rivers of Ethiopia**, which sends ambassadors by sea, Even in vessels of reed on the waters, *saying,* "Go, swift messengers, to **a nation tall and smooth *of skin*,** To a people terrible from their beginning onward, A nation powerful and treading down, **Whose land the rivers divide."**
- **Isaiah 18:7 NKJV:** In that time **a present**

will be brought to the LORD of hosts from a people tall and smooth *of skin*, And from a people terrible from their beginning onward, **A nation powerful and treading down, Whose land the rivers divide—** To the place of the name of the LORD of hosts, To Mount Zion.

- Zephaniah 3:10-14 NKJV: **From beyond the rivers of Ethiopia My worshipers, The daughter of My dispersed ones, Shall bring My offering.** In that day you shall not be shamed for any of your deeds In which you transgress against Me; For then I will take away from your midst Those who rejoice in your pride, And **you shall no longer be haughty In My holy mountain. I will leave in your midst A meek and humble people,** And they shall trust in the name of the LORD. **The remnant of Israel shall do no unrighteousness and speak no lies, Nor shall a deceitful tongue be found in their mouth;** For they shall feed *their* flocks and lie down, And **no one shall make *them* afraid." Sing, O daughter of Zion! Shout, O Israel!** Be glad and rejoice with all *your* heart, O daughter of Jerusalem!

These scriptures speak prophetically of a spiritual people: tall and of smooth skin—symbolically speaking of great spiritual stature and smooth or pure character that will be living in a physical nation beyond the rivers of Ethiopia that will be divided by rivers.

We can see the 'tall stature' and 'smooth skin' symbolizing the perfect church in

- **Ephesians 4:12-13 KJV:** For **the perfecting of the saints**, for the work of the ministry, for the edifying of the body of Christ: Till we all come in the unity of the faith, and of the knowledge of the Son of God, unto a perfect man, **unto the measure of the stature of the fulness of Christ:**
- **Ephesians 5:27 KJV:** That he might present it to himself **a glorious church, not having spot, or wrinkle, or any such thing; but that it should be holy and without blemish.**

Also we can see that this church will be a powerful, militant church that will overcome all its enemies this is shown symbolically in

- **Joel 2:2-3 NKJV:** A day of darkness and

gloominess, A day of clouds and thick darkness, Like the morning *clouds* spread over the mountains. **A people** *come,* **great and strong, the like of whom has never been; Nor will there ever be any** *such* **after them,** Even for many successive generations. A fire devours before them, And behind them a flame burns; The land *is* like the Garden of Eden before them, And behind them a desolate wilderness; **Surely nothing shall escape them.**

Only Nigeria and the church of Jesus Christ in her that is growing into the perfection and fulness of Christ: spiritual Zion fit this unique prophetic description.

The rivers Niger and Benue divide Nigeria.

The church in Nigeria that is growing into the perfection and fulness of Christ is symbolically called Zion and spiritual Israel—the seed of Abraham through the Lord Jesus:

- **Psalms 50:2 NKJV:** Out of Zion, the **perfection of beauty,** God will shine forth.
- **Galatians 3:29 AMP:** And if you belong to Christ [*are in Him Who is Abraham's Seed*],

then you are Abraham's offspring and [*spiritual*] heirs according to promise.

Now because Nigeria and the church in her have this destiny Satan has attacked Nigeria from its political birth in 1960 with bad leadership and legendary, demonically inspired and empowered corruption to try to destroy the nation.

*This is similar to what Satan did when he tried to kill **both Moses (Ex. 1-2) and the Lord Jesus (Mt. 2:16-18)** when they were born because of their strategic prophetic destinies for the saving of Israel and humanity.*

However, just like God saved and preserved both Moses and the Lord Jesus to ultimately fulfill their destines in spite of very unfavourable circumstances (banishment for Moses from Egypt because of murder; military occupation and oppression of Israel by Rome for the Lord Jesus), God is saving and preserving Nigeria so the church in her can grow into perfection and fulness and fulfill her destiny as the **first of the first fruits (Ex.23:19)** of the perfect church in the earth that will ultimately break, rule and disciple both the church and all nations and so **close this age (Mt. 24:14).**

It is instructive to note that the perfect church will

not be in Nigeria alone: it will just be pioneered in Nigeria and then spread to all nations. This is similar to the fact **the birth of the church was pioneered in Israel and later spread to all nations (Acts. 1:8);** and the reformation of the church was pioneered in Germany in 1517 by Martin Luther and later spread to all nations.

So how is God going to save Nigeria at this time of terrible corruption and insecurity that is threatening to destroy the nation?

By destroying selfish and corrupt leaders both spiritual (in the Church) and in the nation and replacing them with righteous leaders.

- **Job 34:20-30 NIV:** They die in an instant, in the middle of the night; the people are shaken and they pass away; **the mighty are removed without human hand.** "His eyes are on the ways of men; he sees their every step. There is no dark place, no deep shadow, where evildoers can hide. God has no need to examine men further, that they should come before him for judgment. Without inquiry **he shatters the mighty and sets up others in their place.** Because he takes note of their deeds, he overthrows them in the night and they are crushed. **He punishes them for their wickedness where everyone can see them,** because they turned from following him and had no regard for any of his ways. They caused the cry of the poor to come before him, so that he heard the cry of the needy. But if he remains silent, who can condemn him? If he hides his face, who can see him? Yet he is over man and nation alike, **to keep a godless man from ruling,** from laying snares for the people.

- **Psalms 144:11-15 KJV:** Rid me, and **deliver me from the hand of strange children,** whose mouth speaketh vanity, and their right hand [is] a right hand of falsehood: That our sons [may be] as plants grown up in their youth; [that] our daughters [may be] as corner stones, polished [after] the similitude of a palace: **That our garners may be full, affording all manner of store: that our sheep may bring forth thousands and ten thousands in our streets: That our oxen may be strong to labour; that there be no breaking in, nor going out; that there be no complaining in our streets. Happy is that people, that is

in such a case: yea, happy is that people, whose God is the LORD.

This divine intervention that will change the leadership of the Church in Nigeria and the nation is imminent: from this year 2013: year of recompense and rest; and onwards.[1]

ZION IN NIGERIA

In his 2018 version of the above sermon (preached on March 4, 2018), Pastor Olubi Johnson expands further:

The church in Nigeria that is growing into the perfection and fulness of Christ is symbolically called Zion and spiritual Israel—the seed of Abraham through the Lord Jesus:

- **Psalms 50:2 NKJV: Out of Zion, the perfection of beauty, God will shine forth.**
- **Galatians 3:29 AMP: And if you belong to Christ [*are in Him Who is Abraham's Seed*], then you are Abraham's offspring and [*spiritual*] heirs according to promise.**
- **Galatians 6:15-16 KJV: For in Christ Jesus neither circumcision availeth any thing,**

nor uncircumcision, but a new creature. And as many as walk according to this rule, peace *be* on them, and mercy, and upon **the Israel of God.**

This Zion church in Nigeria will be the first of the firstfruits of the bride of Christ as shown in

- **Song 1:5-6 KJV: I** *am* **black, but comely,** O ye daughters of Jerusalem, as the tents of Kedar, as the curtains of Solomon. **Look not upon me, because I** *am* **black, because I am darkened by the sun.** My mother's sons were angry with me and made me take care of the vineyards; my own vineyard I had to neglect.

A word of warning must be sounded here. The manifestation of the first of the firstfruits company from beyond the rivers of Ethiopia could become a stumbling block to the rest of the Body of Christ. In the Song of Solomon, the scripture typifies the love relationship between the Lord Jesus Christ and His Church, but especially, the bride of Christ, the perfect Zion Church contained therein in the first six verses are words that will give vital prophetic insight into the nature of the relationship between Christ and His perfect Church.

- **Song 1:1-2 KJV:** The song of songs, which is Solomon's. **Let him kiss me** with a kisses of his mouth: for **thy love is better than wine.**

Now, prophetically speaking, is the time for the individual saints in the Church to come into a place of intimacy with the Lord Jesus (Ps. 2:12) that He may know you and reproduce Himself in you until Christ is formed in you and then birthed (Gal.4: 19; Luke 1:35).

- **Song 1:3 KJV:** Because of the savour of thy good ointments **thy name is as ointment** poured forth, therefore do the virgins love thee.

The Name of the Lord means the same thing as His Character (Exodus 34:5-7) and this is poured forth as the anointing which comes from the Head, **poured out upon the Church flowing out as the Life of God** (Psalm 133). As His Name, or Character is poured forth, those who are wise virgins (Matt. 25) in the Church will be attracted to the beauty of the holiness of the Lord and will therefore love Him (or, obey His commandments, 1 John 5:3).

- **Song 1:4 KJV:** Draw me, **we will run after thee: the king hath brought me into his chambers:** we will be glad and rejoice in thee, we will remember thy love more than wine: **the upright love thee.**

As the fragrance of the Lord's Character draws the wise virgins' attention, they too will begin to run after Him and seek intimacy and fellowship with the Lord until that seeking culminates in the Lord bringing these virgins, or, firstfruits company, into His private chambers, or the Most Holy Place, where intimacy is the order and perfection is attained and manifested.

This attainment of intimacy will bring forth a rejoicing in this firstfruits company. They will be glad and rejoice because now, the marriage supper of the Lamb has come for `His bride' that has **made herself ready (Revelation 19:7).**

- **Song 1:5 KJV: I am black, but comely, O** ye daughters of Jerusalem, as the tents of Kedar, as the curtains of Solomon.

The reason why this first of the firstfruits company is black is because they come from beyond the rivers of Ethiopia, or, tropical, Africa. The black race received the gospel of the Lord Jesus Christ last (in the missionary movements from Europe of the 1700-1900's: the Ethiopian Eunuch of Acts 8 received Christ as an individual but the gospel received then did not lead to a widespread evangelical and discipleship movement beyond the rivers of Ethiopia); but God has ordained that they will be the first to finish the course in perfection;

- **Matthew 20:16 KJV:** So the last shall be first, and the first last:
- **1 Corinthians 1:27-29 KJV:** But **God hath chosen the foolish things of the world to confound the wise: and God hath chosen the weak things of the world to confound the things which are mighty: And base things of the world, and things which are despised, hath God chosen, yea, and things which are not, to bring to nought things that are:** That no flesh should be glory in his presence.

God Himself had decided in His sovereignty to bring the first of the firstfruits of perfection to

Himself from the black race to show forth His righteousness to all races, so that no particular race or nation would have cause to boast in His presence for all have attained their greatness by the mercy and sovereign grace of God.

- **Romans 11:29-32 KJV: For the gifts and calling of God *are* without repentance. For as ye in times past have not believed God, yet have now obtained mercy through their unbelief: Even so have these also now not believed, that through your mercy they also may obtain mercy. For God hath concluded them all in unbelief, that he might have mercy upon all.**

This, therefore, is purely the divine destiny and purpose of the black race that is being fulfilled in this third day by divine sovereignty and mercy.[2]

"SPEAKING UP IS NOT ENOUGH": A WORD TO NIGERIAN YOUTHS

FEW THOUGHTS ON #ENDSARS

JOSEPH OLA

I wrote this post for the membership of the online mentoring platform which my wife and I run — *Alive Mentorship Group* — on 15th October 2020 in the wake of the protests going on in Nigeria at the time by the Nigerian youths. I basically proposed a few practical biblical principles that show how **not** to achieve what I believe the young people are trying to achieve by the protests while offering a few (biblical) thoughts on a better approach.

#IREMEMBER | EPISODE 502 | #ENDSARS

In the past few posts in our #iRemember series, I have been sharing some reflections on a few Proverbs (from 'The Book of Proverbs'). In today's post, I thought to leverage on the ongoing reflection on Proverbs to spotlight a few Proverbs for our consideration particularly with respect to the recent protests in Nigeria which had trended with the hashtag #EndSARS on Twitter. (#EndSARS is a social movement in Nigeria that started on Twitter calling for banning of the Special Anti-Robbery Squad, a unit of the Nigerian Police Force. It is a call to end police oppression and brutality in Nigeria.)

Before I proceed, few disclaimers will be helpful:

1. I am grossly inexperienced in the secular field of Political Science and the related theories about patriotism, nationalism, corporate social responsibility etc. As such, the thoughts I propose in today's post are simply based on scripture. The extent of their contextual application, I reckon, will depend on our understandings and/or experiences of the issues involved and how *each of us* can thus make a difference.

2. I recall being stopped and searched by some uniformed men in 2015 in Lagos around Ojota. My 'crime' was that I crossed the motorway without using the flyover bridge. This led to them ransacking my properties and going through my tablet. They were amazed at how many Christian

books I had on it and engaged me in a long conversation (centred around Romans 13, I kid you not.) I was delayed because I was unwilling to give them what they wanted — a 'bribe'. They were going to put me in an armoured tank and take me to their station at Alausa before one of them decided to 'free' me after seeing my ID Card. Maybe they were SARS. Maybe they weren't; it's all a foggy memory now. I am not unaware, however, that many young people's bitter experience with people of the Force in Nigeria started like that and went south rather quickly. Some of those young people, unfortunately so, did not live to tell their story.

These two disclaimers are meant to highlight how unqualified I am to offer any thought on the protests and violence that had trailed the desire to see things change for the better in my home country. This desire for change, however, is a shared desire, hence, my 'qualification' to offer a thought or two. Besides, we have a Christian responsibility to inveigh injustices. But how, exactly, should we do that? That's my bone of contention in this post.

I have learnt that what we lack in experience, we can make for in the truth of God's Word, and since we've been on a journey through an assortment of reflections from the Book of Proverbs, there is no need to look further for scriptural wisdom on a posture we can take as young people in light of these revolution-in-view protests to end police brutality and its siblings and cousins. The Book of Proverbs is instructive enough. There are proverbs therein on how to have political influence on those in leadership, or to put it like Solomon sometimes put it, "find favour with the king." The key, of course, is WISDOM.

Proverbs 14:35 (AMPC) puts it clearly: *"The KING'S FAVOR is toward a WISE AND DISCREET SERVANT, but his wrath is against him who does shamefully."*

In other words, those who have influence on government are those who are WISE. But what does that look like? Or, to begin with, what does that NOT look like? I think Proverbs 24:21-22 is very instructive in this regard. Here is what it says in a few translations:

— The Message (MSG) *"FEAR GOD, dear child— RESPECT YOUR LEADERS; DON'T BE DEFIANT OR MUTINOUS. Without warning your life can turn upside down, and who knows how or when it might happen?"*

(To be 'mutinous' means "refusing to obey the orders of a person in authority")

— Living Bible (TLB) *"My son, watch your step before the Lord and the king, and DON'T ASSOCIATE WITH RADICALS. For YOU WILL GO DOWN WITH THEM TO SUDDEN DISASTER, and who knows where it all will end?"*

— The Voice (VOICE) *"My son, fear both the Eternal and His anointed ruler. IT IS NOT WISE TO ASSOCIATE WITH THOSE REBELLING AGAINST THEM because disaster can arise from either of them without warning, and who knows what destruction comes down from both of them?"*

In other words, biblical WISDOM in influencing the government — and Solomon did not qualify what nature of government is implied here — is NOT in joining a company of those who are so hell-bent on change that they will defy authority and radically rebel mutinously in pursuit of the change (or worse, personal ulterior motives — whatever those may be). On the contrary, **Solomon offers us a few thoughts on how we can become so influential individually and corporately that even the government of the day will dance** to **our tune.** I will spotlight four of such thoughts, viz:

1. STRIVE TO BE SO COMPETENT THAT YOU RISE TO THE REALM OF POLICY (CHANGE) MAKERS.

Simple, right? Wrong! There is nothing simple about this. Besides, this takes time. While there may be varying degrees of wins from protests (and it goes without saying that any peaceful protest can very easily turn violent in the twinkle of an eye —as, unfortunately, has been the experience of some of the protesters), it's only a matter of time before we are faced with the reality that such wins are more often than none going to birth new challenges. However, Solomon counsels,

"Show me SOMEONE WHO DOES A GOOD JOB, and I will show you someone who is better than most and WORTHY OF THE COMPANY OF KINGS." (Proverbs 22:29 GNT).

"If you are UNIQUELY GIFTED in your work, YOU WILL RISE and be promoted. YOU WON'T BE HELD BACK— you'll stand before kings!" (Proverbs 22:29 TPT).

What does this look like? I think it simply looks like becoming the best at what you do. It looks like subscribing for an endless pursuit of personal development. It looks like positioning ourselves for the inevitable opportunities of tomorrow. Indeed, for the young wo/man who is competent, has a good character and continually acknowledges the grace of God in his/her life, only God knows what can limit such.

2. HAVING A VALID MESSAGE AND SPEAKING UP IS NOT ENOUGH; YOU ALSO NEED TO BE GRACIOUS, PATIENT & TACTFUL.

You see, ordinarily, *"Kings and leaders LOVE TO HEAR GODLY COUNSEL, and they LOVE THOSE WHO TELL THEM THE TRUTH." (Proverbs 16:13 TPT)*. And before you say "that's true everywhere else apart from Nigeria", understand that it is *how* that truth is communicated that determines how the drama will end. To put it as Solomon did, *"Those who LOVE A PURE HEART and SPEAK WITH GRACE will find that THE KING IS THEIR FRIEND." (Proverbs 22:11 VOICE)*.

The one thing that had seemed to be missing from the rhetorics about the recent #EndSARS protest is not TRUTH — most of the arguments I read online are valid and even more so are the true experiences of people; you can't fault that. What I didn't see much of is GRACIOUS communication. (And this transcends this current issue to how we have unconsciously learnt to communicate our opinions in the public sphere by the instrumentality of free social media accounts.)

Yet, the biblical truth is timelessly true: *"He who LOVES PURITY OF HEART and HAS GRACE ON HIS LIPS, The KING WILL BE HIS FRIEND"* (NKJV).

So Solomon came to this conclusion: *"Use PATIENCE and KINDNESS when you want to PERSUADE LEADERS AND WATCH THEM CHANGE THEIR MINDS right in front of you. For YOUR GENTLE WISDOM WILL QUELL THE STRONGEST RESISTANCE."* (Proverbs 25:15 TPT).

Did you say our leaders are HARD-HEADED? *"With patience . . . a gentle word can get through to the HARD-HEADED"* (NCV)

Did you say our leaders are RIGID? *"PATIENT PERSISTENCE pierces through indifference; GENTLE SPEECH   BREAKS*

DOWN **RIGID** DEFENSES." (MSG) Yeah! "By LONG FORBEARANCE AND CALMNESS OF SPIRIT a judge or ruler is persuaded, and SOFT SPEECH BREAKS DOWN THE MOST BONELIKE RESISTANCE." (AMPC)

I could go on and on, but, again, what does this look like? I think it looks like intentionally modelling a new kind of leadership in our respective spheres of influence as young people on the short run—redefining the values we want our nation to be known for and owning it in a practical sense—and on the long run, allowing these new values dictate our engagement in the next (and subsequent rounds of) electoral process. It is refusing to be a victim in the prevalent oppression of corruption and choosing, instead, to acknowledge the tremendous power we have in secret (in prayers, personal development) and in public through practical Christianity, even a wise engagement in the politics of the land.

3. KILL YOUR 'SELF'.

No, I don't mean to commit suicide; I mean to swallow your need for self-assertiveness. If it's all about YOU—wanting YOUR opinion to be heard and YOUR will to be done—you run the risk of being credited with the wages of self-satisfaction, which is DEATH — of whatever sort. That's what landed all of humanity in the quagmire of being born dead — every single one of us — until we encounter the LIFE-giving Saviour.

What Solomon says of someone who has been invited to dine with a King (Proverbs 23:1) is true of how we should deal (generally) with leaders and those in authority — and by acknowledgement of our respective leadership influences, how we should lead. First, he reminds us to "consider (our) manners" (TPT); "mind (our) manners" and "use (our) best manners" (CEV). Then he goes on to remind us of SELF-CONTROL in the next verse. "Control yourself", he says, "if you have a big appetite." (23:2 NCV). Some translations put it even more vividly: "put a knife to your throat" (NIV) — "...do whatever is necessary to curb your enthusiasm for food." (VOICE). [And you can replace 'food' with anything, really. The principle is the same.]

We find it again in Proverbs 25:6-7. *"Don't work yourself into the spotlight..."* (MSG); *"Be not forward (self-assertive...)"* (AMPC). Whatever it is that we do in the public spotlight, it should never be about us.

4. ACKNOWLEDGE THE TRUE KING.

Of one fact, we must never be ignorant: *"THE LORD CONTROLS THE MIND OF A KING as easily as he directs the course of a stream." (Proverbs 21:1 GNT)*.

While we will never have a perfect earthly government as long as sinful men are governing over sinful people, the Sovereign God remains in absolute control! The only perfect system of government is an eschatological anticipation rooted in our blessed hope. But in the meantime, there is nothing stopping God in intervening in the affairs of men. We can achieve much more in our closet in communication with our Father and in public through prophetic prayer walks (in twos or in thousands) than we can in public *mutinous* protests. It's unfortunate how we tend to relegate this privilege to the background when, in fact, it should be our first point of call.

You should never be silent about the injustices in your community — NEVER! But who you speak to about it goes a long way in determining how events will unfold. You've got King Jesus on speed dial; what are you waiting for?

FINAL THOUGHTS

Could it be that we have repeatedly failed to win a hearing from our leaders because we are ignoring these simple principles? Could it be that the reason why we had sometimes been ignored or disregarded is basically that we had not demonstrated competence or civility? Could it be that our words have not been gracious enough, but rather unhelpfully critical or even caustic? May we learn from the models of Daniel and his three Hebrew friends who were very influential in government in spite of being young political prisoners (Daniel 1:17,19-20). May we learn from the model of Joseph who, by virtue of his exceptional wisdom, left behind the injustices that led him into prison to becoming a transformative leader within the same context (Genesis 41:39; 43:32; 46:34). May we be the kind of young adults who grow to be so wise and so skilled that those in government will seek our contribution. And may we be ever-so-tactful in the way we speak and act, thereby influencing the influential. And may we never forget the One Who is truly in charge — whatever form of government we may live under.

Amen.

O God of creation,

Direct our noble cause;
Guide our Leaders right:
Help our Youth the truth to know,
In love and honesty to grow,
And living just and true,
Great lofty heights attain,
To build a nation where peace and justice reign.

Amen.

PS: #iRemember is a daily mentoring retrospective look at Chronicles of our past—my wife and I—drawing life lessons from past experiences. It is exclusive to members of Alive Mentorship Group—an online mentorship platform for young adults across the world that provides an avenue to learn practical life lessons across geographical barriers. If you will like to be a part, or to access any of our free resources, visit https://linktr.ee/josephola.

NOTES

PREFACE

1. Written by Whitney Smith, Director, Flag Research Center, Winchester, Massachusetts and the author of "Flags and Arms Around the World". https://www.britannica.com/topic/flag-of-Nigeria [Emphasis mine].
2. From NCCF Adamawa State Website. https://adamawanccf.wordpress.com/our-history/ [accessed September 15, 2020]
3. For the records, I hate the word 'denomination' but have to use it for want of a better term.

1. 1792-1888

1. See William Carey, *An Enquiry into the Obligations of Christians to Use Means for the Conversion of the Heathens* (London: Carey Kingsgate, 1961).
2. Harvey C. Kwiyani, *Multicultural Kingdom: Ethnic Diversity, Mission and the Church.* London, UK: SCM Press, 2020, 19. For more on 'Blessed reflex', see Kenneth R. Ross, "Blessed Reflex" : Mission as God's Spiral of Renewal', *International Bulletin of Missionary Research* 27, no. 4 (2003).
3. *Multicultural Kingdom*, 19.
4. Edward Wilmot Blyden, *Christianity, Islam and the Negro Race* (Baltimore: Black Classic, 1888), p. 143.
5. John Jea, *The Life, History and Unparalleled Sufferings of John Jea, The African Preacher* (Cornwall: Dodo Press, 2009).

6. David Killingray, "The Black Atlantic Missionary Movement and Africa", *Journal of Religion in Africa*, 33.1 (2003), 3-31 <https://doi.org/10.1163/157006603765626695>.

7. Now known as Sureway International Christian Ministries, Herne Hill, South East London. "Sureway International Christian Ministries", *Sureway International Christian Ministries*<http://www.surewayministries.org/> [accessed 3 October 2017].

8. Marika Sherwood, *Pastor Daniels Ekarte And the African Churches Mission Liverpool 1931-1964* (London: Savannah Press, 1994).

9. Hereafter referred to as ACM

10. From documents from Nigerian National Archives in Ibadan, Higgins deduced that Ekarte began his ministry near the Liverpool docks in 1922. See Thomas Winfield Higgins, "Mission Networks and The African Diaspora in Britain", *African Diaspora*, 5.2 (2012), 165-186 <https://doi.org/10.1163/18725457-12341236>.

11. Quoted in Thomas Winfield Higgins, "Mission Networks And The African Diaspora In Britain", *African Diaspora*, 5.2 (2012), 165-186 <https://doi.org/10.1163/18725457-12341236>.

12. It is worthy of note that Toxteth where the African Churches Mission was located is still the preferred location of APCs in Liverpool as the history of the area both before and after the days of Daniels Ekarte is rich in the involvements of the ethnic minority. See "History of Toxteth", *Historic Liverpool* <http://historic-liverpool.co.uk/toxteth/> [accessed 2 September 2017].

13. Marika Sherwood, pp. 32ff.

14. This migration of Europeans to different parts of the world led to over 20% of European population relocated elsewhere mainly for economic reasons. See Harvey C Kwiyani, *Mission-Shaped Church in A Multicultural World* (Oxford, UK: Grove Books Ltd, 2017), p. 13.

15. Israel Olofinjana, *Partnership in Mission* (Wartford: Instant Apostle, 2015), p. 26.

16. William Doe Kugbeadjor and Harvey Kwiyani, "Exploring Adaptive Challenges Faced by African Missionaries in Britain: The Case of The Church of Pentecost", *Missio Africanus Journal of African Missiology*, 1.2 (2016), 4-15.

17. Or Independent, Instituted, Indigenous (and lately, International). They are the churches that began the indigenisation of Christianity in Africa as a revolt against European Christianity introduced by the Mission Churches.

18. Israel Olofinjana, *Partnership in Mission* (Wartford: Instant Apostle, 2015), p. 26.

19. Ibid.

20. Richard Burgess, "Bringing back the gospel: Reverse mission among Nigerian Pentecostals in Britain." *Journal of Religion in Europe* 4, no. 3 (2011): 429-449.

2. 1970-1980

1. Ayodeji Abodunde, *Messenger: Sydney Elton and the Making of Pentecostalism in Nigeria*. Pierce Watershed, 2016, 378.

3. 1983

1. Intercessors For Nigeria, "Prophecies Concerning Nigeria." *Intercessors For Nigeria*, June 5, 2014, https://intercessorsfornigeria.org/prophecies-concerning-nigeria/ [accessed September 15, 2020]

2. *Ibid.*

3. *Ibid.*

4. 1984

1. Intercessors For Nigeria, "Prophecies Concerning Nigeria." *Intercessors For Nigeria,* June 5, 2014, https:// intercessorsfornigeria.org/prophecies-concerning-nigeria/ [accessed September 15, 2020]

5. 1986

1. Isaac Ezeh, *God's Eternal Plan for Nigeria: Seven Eras of the Nation.* Independently published, 2017, back cover.
2. Very Rev Dr Deji Okegbile, "Remembering Pa Elton", May 21, 2017. http://dejiokegbile.com/remembering-pa-elton/

6. 1989

1. Intercessors For Nigeria, "Prophecies Concerning Nigeria." *Intercessors For Nigeria,* June 5, 2014, https:// intercessorsfornigeria.org/prophecies-concerning-nigeria/ [accessed September 15, 2020]

7. 1990

1. M. O. Ojewale, A Call to Prayer for Nigeria (Lagos: Peace and Salvation Publishers, 1990), 23–24, 37

8. 1996

1. Intercessors For Nigeria, "Prophecies Concerning Nigeria." *Intercessors For Nigeria*, June 5, 2014, https:// intercessorsfornigeria.org/prophecies-concerning-nigeria/ [accessed September 15, 2020]
2. Romans 2:24
3. The Voice Bible Copyright © 2012 Thomas Nelson, Inc. The Voice™ translation © 2012 Ecclesia Bible Society All rights reserved.
4. Habakkuk 1:5

9. 1998

1. J. Lee Grady, "Nigeria's Miracle," cover story, *Charisma*, May 2002, 4.
2. Ruth Marshall, *Political Spiritualities: The Pentecostal Revolution in Nigeria*. Chicago: University of Chicago Press, 2009, 217.
3. J. Lee Grady, "Nigeria's Miracle," cover story, *Charisma*, May 2002, 4.

10. 2000

1. Intercessors For Nigeria, "Prophecies Concerning Nigeria." *Intercessors For Nigeria*, June 5, 2014, https:// intercessorsfornigeria.org/prophecies-concerning-nigeria/ [accessed September 15, 2020]
2. *Ibid.*
3. *Ibid.*
4. *Ibid.*

11. 2002

1. Intercessors For Nigeria, "Prophecies Concerning Nigeria." *Intercessors For Nigeria,* June 5, 2014, https://intercessorsfornigeria.org/prophecies-concerning-nigeria/ [accessed September 15, 2020]

12. 2005

1. Intercessors For Nigeria, "Prophecies Concerning Nigeria." *Intercessors For Nigeria,* June 5, 2014, https://intercessorsfornigeria.org/prophecies-concerning-nigeria/ [accessed September 15, 2020]

13. 2011

1. Gbenga Richmond, *Grineria: End of the Old; Birth of the New.* AuthorHouse UK, 2012, 33-34.

14. 2014

1. Shared with me by email correspondence from Pastor Olaoluwa Okunnuwa, October 2020.

15. 2015

1. Dr David Jonathan, *Prophetic Word For New Nigeria – Part 1* http://www.jonathan-david.org/sermon/propheticwordnewnigeria-2/ [As transcribed by the author.]
2. Dr David Jonathan, *Prophetic Word For New Nigeria – Part 2* https://youtu.be/s9GYeUsSUT4 [As transcribed by the

author.]

16. 2016

1. Olubi Johnson, "Week 04, Jan 2016 | Building Up Zion From Beyond The Rivers of Ethiopia" https://www.spcconline3.net/2016/09/week-04-jan-2016-building-up-zion-from-beyond-the-rivers-of-ethiopia/
2. As shared on Facebook by Pastor Debo Adesina on 25 October: https://www.facebook.com/debo.adesina.3/posts/37099306622352882

17. 2017

1. Jeremiah 29:11
2. The G7 Nations
3. Joseph Olowe, *Vision 2030: The Rebirth of Nigeria.* Independently Published, 2019, 2-5.

18. 2020

1. Shared with me by email correspondence from Pastor Olaoluwa Okunnuwa, October 2020.
2. Shared with me by email correspondence from Pastor Olaoluwa Okunnuwa, October 2020.
3. Peace House Gboko [Facebook Page], *Prophetic Declaration for Nigeria,* https://www.facebook.com/160372541210935/videos/355594002523811/ [As transcribed by the author.]
4. Shared with me by email correspondence from Pastor Olaoluwa Okunnuwa, October 2020.

PA S.G. ELTON: A TRIBUTE

1. Ayodeji Abodunde, *Messenger: Sydney Elton and the Making of Pentecostalism in Nigeria.* Pierce Watershed, 2016, 3-6.

A CALL TO ORDER

1. Ruth Marshall, *Political Spiritualities: The Pentecostal Revolution in Nigeria.* Chicago: University of Chicago Press, 2009, 217.
2. Dr. Tony Rapu, "A Call to Order." 2002. See http://www.thispresenthouse.org/home/firstword.cfm?ContentID=241

SAVING NIGERIA

1. Olubi Johnson, "Week 10, Mar 2013 | Saving Nigeria" https://www.spcconline3.net/2016/09/week-10-mar-2013-saving-nigeria/
2. Olubi Johnson, "03, Mar 2018 | Zion in Nigeria" https://www.spcconline3.net/2018/03/03-mar-2018-zion-in-nigeria-2/

WAITING COMPASS: FINDING GOD WHEN HE SEEMS TO DELAY

Waiting Compass: Finding God when He seems to delay

WHERE IS THE ALL-POWERFUL GOD?

If God is so loving and all-powerful, how come He is missing in inaction? How come He's silent to my legitimate requests? He promised that none of His shall be barren. Where is the baby? He promised that the prayer of faith will heal the sick. Why am I still sick? He promised to answer before I call. Where is the answer after calling and calling again? **WHERE IS GOD?**

It's a question you've probably asked. It's a question Joseph has definitely asked when his reality seemed decades away from what God had promised. Thus, in five 'peaces' of transformational thoughts, Joseph hands us a compass which points us in the direction where God may be found in times like that. With lots of stories from his personal journey, Joseph writes with such simplicity and clarity that drives home the message and leaves the seeker immersed in the unwavering hope of God's reassuring promise: "I will never leave you, nor forsake you."

#UNADDICTED: FINDING FREEDOM FROM SEX-RELATED ADDICTIONS

#Unaddicted: Finding Freedom from Sex-related Addictions

In his years of engaging with teenagers and young adults, the question Joseph has been most frequently asked is on **overcoming sexual addictions—especially pornography and masturbation.**

This book brings together in one volume Joseph's liberating thoughts on how to do this, sharing unreservedly from his journey through the same struggles.

The book is easy-to-read and has been a helpful resource for many teenagers and young adults.

BUMPY BUT SWEET | A LOVE STORY: LESSONS LEARNT ON FINDING A LIFE PARTNER AND BUILDING A GODLY RELATIONSHIP

Bumpy But Sweet | A Love Story: LESSONS LEARNT ON FINDING A LIFE PARTNER AND BUILDING A GODLY RELATIONSHIP

Anu married Joseph on the same day she graduated with a First Class from her LLB degree. Their marriage story went viral on the internet partly for the unique combination of marrying and graduating on a single day and partly because of their incredible love story. This ebook details an up-close-and-personal look into their love story initially shared on an online seminar. They answered lots of questions from young adults about love, dating, courtship, sex, and discerning the will of God besides many other elements that constitute a godly marriage. The book has been a very helpful resource to thousands of singles and young couples.

IS THIS OPPORTUNITY FROM GOD?: 7 CHECKPOINTS FOR DISCERNING DIVINE OPPORTUNITIES

Is This Opportunity From God?: 7 Checkpoints for Discerning Divine Opportunities

The difference between joy and regret sometimes is being able to discern between what is *good* and what is *God*.

We will be faced with many opportunities in life, but how can we tell which of them is not a distraction from God's best plan for us? In this book, reflecting on scripture and personal experience, Joseph lays out 7 checkpoints to help the reader discern if an opportunity is indeed from God or just another distraction from His best plan. In this book you will learn:

- How to avoid regret

- Positive and negative signs to watch out for in making a choice

- Tips on choosing a life partner…and lots more!

MARRIAGE IN VIEW: READY? SLEEP. GO!

Marriage in View: Ready? Sleep. Go!

This book will surely save many young adults from unnecessary heartbreak.

Besides coming into a relationship with God, there is hardly any decision that is of more significance and long-lasting implications than the decision on who to marry. With the increasing misrepresentation of marriage through popular culture, young people are desperate for trustworthy models and principles to guide them through the waters of marriage-in-view relationships, hence this book. Joseph and Anu, through their love story, draw young people to engage with the tested and timeless countercultural principles upon which the institution of marriage is established. Written in a warm and conversational style, the book will teach you:

- guidelines on discovering who to marry;
- answers to questions about dating, courtship, sex and
  weddings; and

- principles for building a Godly marriage.

PANDEMIC JOY: MAKING SENSE OF LIFE'S UNCERTAINTIES

Pandemic Joy: Making Sense of Life's Uncertainties

In this book, Joseph Ola tackles the tricky and very immediate subject of making sense of life's uncertainties as Christians. His contribution is steeped in his reading of scripture and theology interwoven with some thoughtfully chosen Yoruba proverbs and practical illustrations from everyday life. At its core, the book reminds us to live wisely as good citizens whilst holding steadfastly to the joy that belongs to those who follow the way of the risen Christ. For readers who sense they are living in anxious times, this book offers practical wisdom shot through with the joy of the gospel. — **Colin Smith | Dean of Mission Education, Church Mission Society, Oxford**

"An excellent read for anyone struggling to make sense of the uncertainties of life." — **Rev Canon Elaine Jones | Vicar, Church of England, UK.**

"They say a book is only as good as the timing it lands in your world and I would say that this is a timely book for many!" — **Rich Martin | Principal, LIFE Church UK College**

"Rarely is a book quite as topical or as encouraging as Joseph Ola's Pandemic Joy." — **John Neate | Vineyard Churches, UK**

YOUNG AND FOUND: A 40-DAY DEVOTIONAL FOR YOUNG ADULTS AND TEENS

Young and Found: A 40-Day Devotional for Young Adults and Teens

You Don't Belong To 'a Lost Generation'!

It is unfortunate that today's young adults and teens have been labeled *'a lost generation'*. **To be *young*, in the eyes of popular media, is to be *lost*.** But this does not have to be the case. Reflecting on their life experiences and the honest questions they have been asked by teenagers and young adults, Joseph and Anu share practical and biblical wisdom on the complex everyday challenges that young Christians face. Subjects covered include: *personal development, hearing God's voice, sex and sexuality, parent-youth relationships, faith, integrity, fun, marriage, managing weaknesses, prayer, pioneering, time and money management* — to mention but a few. Each day's reflection is accompanied with practical tips on applying the message and a prayer. These reflections have already helped thousands of millennials realise that they are young but not lost; **they are *young and found* in Christ.** It is the authors' prayer that this becomes the testimony of everyone who reads this.

Inspired by what you just read?
Connect with Joseph.

Follow Joseph's teaching ministry, Word Alive, online.
Visit www.JosephKolawole.org to get FREE resources for your
spiritual growth and encouragement, including:

Blog Posts
Downloads of video, audio, and printed material
Joseph's podcast
First look at book excerpts
Mobile content.
You will also find an eStore and special offers.

Follow Joseph on Twitter @iamJosephOla
Or at Facebook.com/JosephKolawole